JOAN OF ARC

OF FIRE AND OF BLOOD

Story:
EHO

Illustrations:
PAILLOU

Colours:
Claire DUMAS

The authors and the editor would like to particularly thank
Alain Préaux, for his precious advice and for drafting
the interchapter texts, and Olivier Bouzy, for his historic insight
and his contribution to the appendix contents.

This project has benefited from support from the Normandy Regional
Council, the Regional Cultural Affairs Directorate and the Centre National
du Livre, within the framework of the FADEL Normandie development fund.

OREP Éditions, Zone tertiaire de Nonant, 14400 BAYEUX
Tel: 02 31 51 81 31 - ***Fax:*** 02 31 51 81 32
E-mail: info@orepeditions.com - ***Web:*** www.orepeditions.com

Graphic design: OREP
Joan of Arc logotype, lettering and layout: David Thouroude
Credits: back cover, Joan of Arc's signature ©Archives municipales, Reims.
English translation: Heather Inglis, Tina Levaudel
ISBN: 978-2-8151-0297-1

Legal deposit: 1st quarter 2017

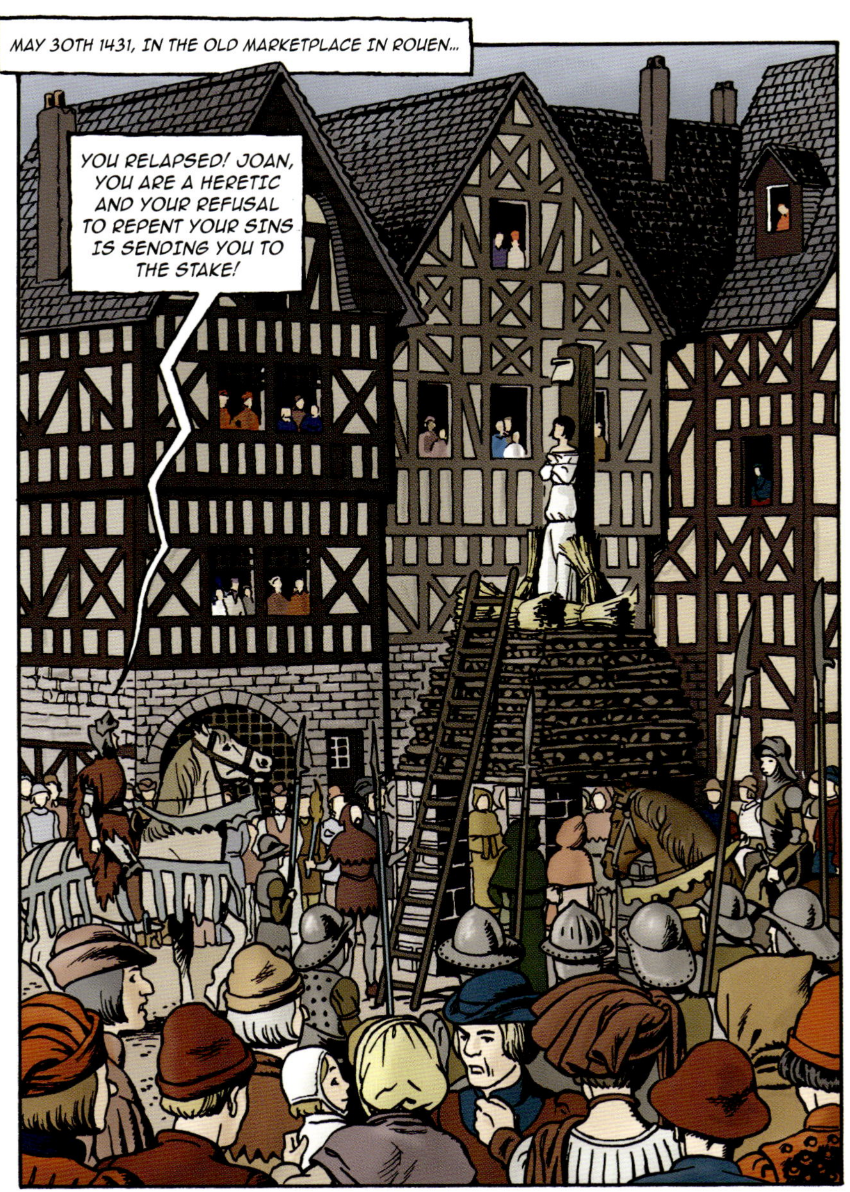
MAY 30TH 1431, IN THE OLD MARKETPLACE IN ROUEN...
YOU RELAPSED! JOAN, YOU ARE A HERETIC AND YOUR REFUSAL TO REPENT YOUR SINS IS SENDING YOU TO THE STAKE!

GOD! HAVE YOU NOTHING TO SAY? YOU STILL HAVE TIME!

I ONLY WANT ONE THING, ENGLISHMAN...
GIVE ME A CRUCIFIX, THAT IT MAY GUIDE ME TOWARDS THE LORD.

DAMN! NO ONE CAN ACCUSE ME OF NOT HAVING DONE MY ALL TO SAVE HER!
SOLDIER, GIVE HER THE CRUCIFIX...
AND LET'S BE DONE!

FORGIVE ME JOAN, I AM BUT FOLLOWING ORDERS...

TAKE THIS CRUCIFIX: MAY IT LESSEN YOUR FEARS AND PROTECT YOU FROM THE FINAL JUDGEMENT...

MY VOICES...
MY VERY DEAR VOICES...
GUIDE ME TO HEAVEN, MY LORD...

GUIDE ME...
... AS YOU ALWAYS HAVE, SINCE DOMREMY, SINCE I WAS JUST THIRTEEN...
SINCE THAT VERY FIRST DAY...

DOMREMY, 1425
HAUVIETTE, HAUVIETTE! IT'S MARVELLOUS!
JOAN?!

I WAS GIVING SOME WATER TO THE SHEEP NEAR THE GARDEN AND SUDDENLY HE APPEARED TO ME! HE WAS SO HANDSOME AND SO GREAT!
WHO WAS HANDSOME? WHO WAS GREAT? I DON'T HAVE A CLUE WHAT YOU'RE TALKING ABOUT...
SAINT MICHAEL, THE ARCHANGEL! HE CAME DOWN TO EARTH TO TALK WITH ME, ALL SWATHED IN LIGHT! IT WAS MAGNIFICENT!

HE HAS ORDERED ME TO BEHAVE WELL AND TO LIVE FOR THE LORD! AND ALSO...
?!
HE HAS ENTRUSTED ME WITH A MISSION!

A MISSION? AN ARCHANGEL?!
TAKE MY ADVICE AND KEEP THAT SECRET...
YOU COULD BE TAKEN FOR A WITCH AND THAT COULD COST YOU YOUR LIFE!

IN 1428
JOAN, JOAN...
THREE YEARS HAVE GONE BY...

YOU CAN NO LONGER STAY IN THE SHADOWS. YOU CAN NO LONGER KEEP THIS ALL TO YOURSELF...
YOUR VILLAGE, DOMREMY, HAS ALREADY SUFFERED ENOUGH FROM THE BARBARIAN INVASIONS...

BUT, SAINT MICHAEL...

ORLEANS IS BESIEGED BY THE ENGLISH...

GO AND FIND CHARLES, THE NOBLE DAUPHIN AND GUIDE HIM TO THE THRONE...
SAINT CATHERINE AND SAINT MARGARET ARE BY YOUR SIDE! THE TIME HAS COME TO ACCOMPLISH YOUR MISSION... TO SAVE THE KINGDOM OF FRANCE!

SAINT MICHAEL THE ARCHANGEL, YOU HAVE NOW CHOSEN ME...

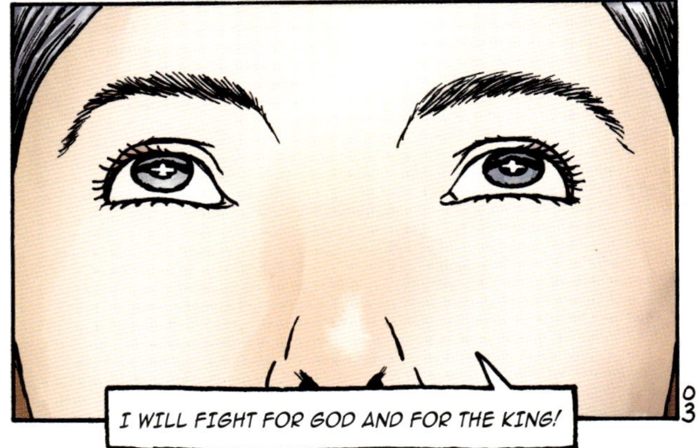
I WILL FIGHT FOR GOD AND FOR THE KING!

VAUCOULEURS, FEBRUARY 1429
LORD OF BEAUDRICOURT, THE GIRL IS BACK! SHE IS HERE, IN VAUCOULEURS, AND SHE ASKS TO SPEAK WITH YOU.
LET'S BE DONE! DO AS YOU WISH, LET HER ENTER OR THROW HER OUT!

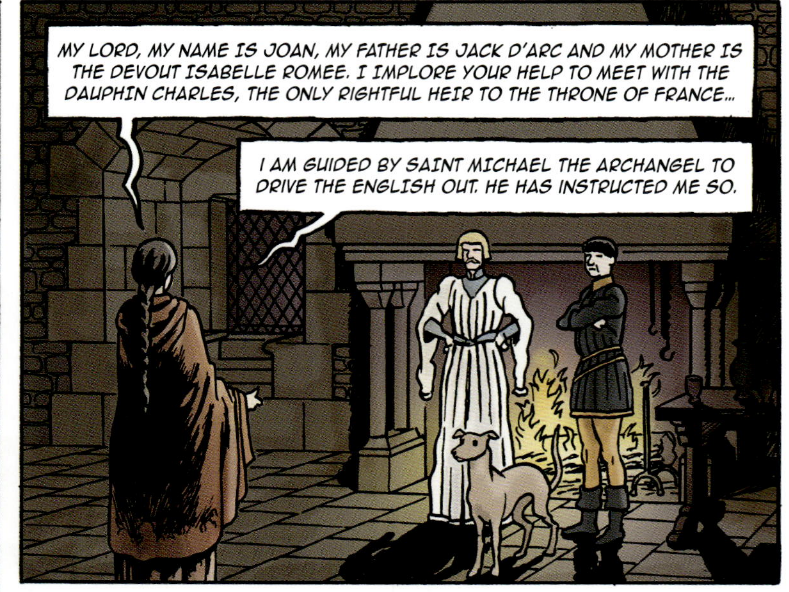
MY LORD, MY NAME IS JOAN, MY FATHER IS JACK D'ARC AND MY MOTHER IS THE DEVOUT ISABELLE ROMEE. I IMPLORE YOUR HELP TO MEET WITH THE DAUPHIN CHARLES, THE ONLY RIGHTFUL HEIR TO THE THRONE OF FRANCE...
I AM GUIDED BY SAINT MICHAEL THE ARCHANGEL TO DRIVE THE ENGLISH OUT. HE HAS INSTRUCTED ME SO.

WHAT DO YOU THINK, POULENGY? IS SHE EARNEST OR DO YOU SEE IN THIS SOME KIND OF WITCHCRAFT?!
WELL...

IF I DO NOTHING, THE KINGDOM OF FRANCE WILL BE OVERWHELMED BY DARKNESS AND SORROW...
... INVADED AND CRUSHED BY THE ENGLISH AND THEIR DAMNED SOULS - THOSE FOUL BURGUNDIANS!

LISTEN TO HER MY LORD, FOR HER WORDS COME NOT FROM HER MOUTH BUT FROM HER HEART.

THEN LET US ARM THIS YOUNG WOMAN AND ESCORT HER WITH SIX OF MY BEST MEN THAT SHE MAY GO AND MEET THE DAUPHIN...
... AND COME WHAT MAY!

JOHN, DON'T YOU BELIEVE ME? DARE YOU SUGGEST THAT I AM LYING? THAT I DO NOT HEAR THOSE VOICES?
FOR THE LOVE OF GOD, OF COURSE I BELIEVE YOU!

ALL I AM SAYING IS THAT OUR DAUPHIN HAS NEITHER MONEY NOR REASON TO RAISE TROOPS.

IT WILL COST HIM NOTHING TO RECEIVE ME...

I MUST TELL HIM HE IS THE CHOSEN ONE!

MAY I MEET HIM JUST FOR A MOMENT!

HE WILL LISTEN TO ME!

CHINON, LATE FEBRUARY...
THE KING IS INDECISIVE, JOAN...
WE CAN BUT UNDERSTAND...
OTHERS HAVE COME BEFORE YOU, SUPPOSEDLY RECOMMENDED BY GOD, YET THE SITUATION HAS NOT IMPROVED FOR AS MUCH!

YOUR TENACITY HAS PAID OFF, JOAN, LOOK! HERE YOU ARE BEFORE CHARLES...
MY LORD, MY NAME IS JOAN AND I AM YOUR SERVANT...
?!
I HAVE BEEN CHOSEN BY GOD TO RAISE THE SIEGE OF ORLEANS AND TO LEAD YOU TO THE THRONE OF FRANCE AND THE ANOINTMENT.
REALLY?? WHAT DO YOU WISH TO SAY TO ME?
I MUST TALK TO YOU BUT WHAT I HAVE TO SAY IS FOR YOUR EARS ONLY...
I WOULD SELL MY SOUL TO THE DEVIL FOR A SNIPPET OF WHAT THAT GIRL IS TELLING HIM!
DO NOT BLASPHEME, MY SON, IT IS SAID THAT THE GIRL HAS GREAT POWERS!
THANK YOU, JOAN. YOU BRING ME GREATER PROSPECTS.
GO IMMEDIATELY TO THE UNIVERSITY OF POITIERS AND IF YOU CONVINCE THE CLERGYMEN AS YOU HAVE CONVINCED ME, YOU MAY LEAD MY ARMY.
YOU SEEM TROUBLED, CHARLES, COULD THIS YOUNG WOMAN BE OF HELP TO YOU?
I HAVE NEWFOUND HOPE... WHAT SHE HAS TOLD ME IS KNOWN ONLY TO GOD...
TO GOD... AND TO THE DEVIL!

Domremy

The name of Domremy comes from *Domus Remigius*, the oldest mention of which dates back to the founding act of the Châtenois Priory in 1070. In the 15th century, the village was more important than it is today for, at the time, the parish comprised both Domremy and Greux (which were separated in 1820). Domremy stretched over a surface area of 864 hectares on the left bank of the River Meuse and it comprised 35 homes. The village of Domremy was shared between several authorities: the northern part, including the castle and the rest of the village, belonged to the *Barrois mouvant* (territories located in Lorraine and under the dependency of the King of France), whereas the southern part, including Joan's birthplace and the church, was dependent upon the Mureaux Abbey and came under the Kingdom of France.

'My father was named Jack of Arc, and my mother Isabelle...' He was a wealthy peasant, even if he *'was not very rich.'* A labourer, he owned his own plough, which was by no means incompatible with his status as a serf of the Mureaux Abbey. With another inhabitant, he shared, by halves, the rent of the castle 'of the island' (fortified house), which he used to store grain. He acted as dean (the mayor's deputy) and was appointed *'procurator of the inhabitants'* during a trial before Robert de Baudricourt (Captain of Vaucouleurs in the Duchy of Bar).

Joan grew up just like all the other village children with her brothers and her sister (Jack, Catherine, John and Peter). She joined the other girls and boys in play in the surrounding area. Despite her lack of writing or reading skills, her mother gave her instruction on her 'faith', teaching her prayers and certain psalms.

Every day, she helped her parents work in the fields, occasionally taking her father's herd to the communal pastures. She drove the plough animals during harvests and, with the women and other children, Joan walked behind the harvesters to gather the sheaves that the men then piled up in huge stacks. One can presume that, like all other children at the time, she also took advantage of the presence of horses to enjoy a ride on the way back from the harvest; knowing how to ride was to be of use to her later, in particular when she met with the Duke of Lorraine who asked her to heal him from an illness. During this encounter, Joan told him she, *'knew nothing'* of the subject and that if he wished to recover, he must return to his wife, leaving the young mistress he had taken. Vexed, the duke gave her four francs and a black horse before instantly dismissing her.

This image is far from that of the young shepherdess who kept the sheep in the 'bois chenu' woods (in Domremy, where a basilica devoted to Joan of Arc now stands).

In the family home, from a very young age, Joan and her sister Catherine set to the women's chores, in particular spinning yarn, doing housework, cooking, gardening, feeding the animals, etc. She later told, during her trial, *'In sewing and spinning, I fear no woman in Rouen.'*

Life in the village also included its lot of distractions. Evening congregations when they listened to the itinerant monks or some other traveller. And of course, in the spring and summer, there were gatherings to feast under the shade of the Ladies' tree, also known as the Fairies' tree. This Ladies' tree was in fact a magnificent beech, *'as beautiful as a lily with branches and leaves as far as the ground'.* In the summer, the children climbed up the hill to the fountain,where they ate their small bread and drank fresh water; then they danced in circles and sang songs before heading home over a pleasant walk.

Joan was a young girl from a relatively wealthy family – necessary to feed five children – whose parents kept a watchful eye on, *'Her father and mother took great care in keeping her, holding her under great subjection; and she obeyed them in all circumstances...'*

Depositions made during her trial told of how she occasionally isolated herself to pray or to listen to her voices. Joan was a good, chaste, simple and reserved young girl, cursing neither God nor his saints, but fearing him, regularly attending church and confessing.

Joan was 13 years old in July 1425 when a troop of Burgundians came to Domremy to steal livestock. The animals were recovered; however, fear was rife and the decision was made to take refuge in Neufchâteau. When danger struck, it was commonplace for country folk to take refuge with the lord of the land, since the inhabitants of the outskirts of his territory – where the 'seigneur' exerted his political power, known as the 'power of the ban' – contributed towards the construction of the ramparts. In return, he offered them protection.

SO YOU CONVINCED THE DAUPHIN... I AM MOST IMPRESSED, JOAN!
I MUST ADMIT, I WAS DOUBTFUL.
GOD AND HIS ANGELS ARE BY MY SIDE, LA HIRE MY LOYAL FRIEND.
MY QUEST IS JUST, OF THAT CHARLES IS SURE.

I HAVE HAD A MISSIVE SENT TO THE ENGLISH. THEY HAVE BEEN WARNED...

THE DUKE OF BEDFORD AND HIS TROOPS MUST LEAVE AND GIVE UP THE SIEGE OF ORLEANS, OTHERWISE I WILL SEND THEM BACK TO THEIR CURSED ISLAND...

IT WILL SOON BE SETTLED, FOR HERE COMES YOUR MESSENGER!

SO?
SO, THEY LAUGHED JOAN, THEY LAUGHED!

AT NO COST WILL THEY ABANDON ORLEANS, AND THEY ARE STARVING THE PEOPLE!
VERY WELL! SAINT MICHAEL, GUIDE ME THAT I MAY DRIVE THE ENGLISH OUT OF FRANCE!

JOAN'S CONVOY SOON ARRIVES ON THE BANKS OF THE RIVER LOIRE, WHERE SUPPLIES FOR ORLEANS HAVE BEEN BOARDED.
HERE ARE THE BOATS WE MUST ESCORT...
SHE'S HERE! SHE'S HERE! THE MAID IS COMING!
!!!
SO, THIS IS THE YOUNG WOMAN SENT BY GOD?
WELCOME CHILD!
AND WITHOUT A DOUBT, YOU MUST BE THE BASTARD OF ORLEANS... HE WHO, FOR THE PAST SIX MONTHS, HAS FAILED TO RAISE THE SIEGE ON HIS CITY...
VALOUR DOES NOT DEPEND UPON AGE... WHAT IS THE SITUATION WITH THE ENGLISH?
WE HAVE SENT TROOPS TO CREATE A DIVERSION AND KEEP THEM BUSY AT THE SAINT-LOUP BASTILLE...
THE ROAD IS CLEAR...
BUT WITH THESE STRONG HEAD WINDS, THE CONVOY WILL NEVER MAKE IT TO ORLEANS!
KEEP FAITH MY FRIEND...

THE WIND, THE WIND! IT IS CHANGING DIRECTION!
IT'S A MIRACLE!
QUICK, COME ABOARD!
JOAN, LET YOUR TROOPS GO TO BLOIS TO GET THE ROYAL ARMY AND COME WITH ME TO ORLEANS!
BUT I...
HE IS RIGHT JOAN, YOUR PLACE IS HERE!
... AND THE GATES OF ORLEANS, CLOSED FOR SIX MONTHS, OPEN UP TO LET JOAN ENTER...
WHAT A WELCOME! I HAVE NOT SEEN THE PEOPLE OF ORLEANS SO JOYFUL FOR A LONG LONG TIME!
JOAN!
JOAN!
GOD BE WITH US!
YOU BRING THEM RENEWED FAITH...
AND TO ME, BY YOUR SIDE...
I AM SURE WE WILL FREE THE CITY OF ORLEANS...
Auberge
I KNOW IT...
I CAN FEEL IT!

THE ENGLISH HAVE ENCIRCLED ALMOST THE ENTIRE CITY: THESE VILLAINS HAVE BESIEGED THE SAINT-LOUP AND THE AUGUSTINS BASTILLES, THE TOURELLES GATEHOUSE TOO.

IT IS WITHIN THE LATTER THAT THE DASTARDLY CAPTAIN GLASDALE HAS SET UP HIS HEADQUARTERS...

WELL, WE WILL JUST HAVE TO FORCE THE DEVIL OUT OF HIS LAIR...

Ihesus Maria Ihesus Maria
TOMORROW WE WILL START A PROCESSION TO FREE THE CITY OF ORLEANS...
... THEN, WITH THE HELP OF GOD, WE WILL GO TO THE TOURELLES...

... AND WE WILL FORCE THEM TO SURRENDER!
FOR THE KING... AND FOR FRANCE!

BUT THE FOLLOWING DAY, AT THE FOOT OF THE TOURELLES GATEHOUSE...

GLASDALE!
CAR JE N'AI QU'UN HÉRITIER

BY THE GRACE OF GOD, SURRENDER, BOTH YOU AND YOUR MEN... AND WE WILL SPARE YOU ALL!
OH, REALLY?

GOSH! POOR WORTHLESS GIRL...

BE GONE COWGIRL!
BE GONE!

IF WE CATCH YOU, WE WILL BURN YOU!

BLASTED FOOL! YOU WILL REGRET THESE WORDS! FOR PITY'S SAKE! DO YOU NOT REALISE WHAT YOU RISK?!
IN THREE DAYS, WE WILL BE JOINED BY THE ROYAL ARMY AND YOUR BAND OF UNGODLY ROGUES WILL BE DECIMATED!
SOLDIERS! WE WILL CLEAR THIS PLACE OF THIS ENGLISH SCUM!
AND SHOULD THEY NOT YIELD, THEN LET THEM IMPLORE GOD'S PITY!
AT DAWN, ON THE 4TH OF MAY, THE FIRST ASSAULT IS LAUNCHED...
TO THE BASTILLE OF SAINT-LOUP!

The Hundred Years' War

In 1328, when, against all expectations, the direct Capetian lineage disappeared with the successive deaths of Philip the Fair's three sons, France chose Philip, Count of Valois, as its king, against Edward III of England, who was the deceased king's nephew.

In January 1340, stating his claims to the French legacy, Edward II took the title of 'King of France' and had the fleur-de-lis added to his coat of arms. Shortly afterwards, a new series of conflicts began between these two traditionally enemy nations (for example, when, in 1066, the Duke of Normandy became 'William the Conqueror', King of England), conflict that was marked by a number of costly defeats for France: Crécy and Calais (1346), Poitiers (1356) then Azincourt (1415)... It was the Hundred Years' War. Misery was rife with the great 1315-1316 famine in the West and, of course, the devastation caused by the Plague in 1348. It was also a period of social unrest resulting in many revolts: the Harelle in Rouen, the Tuchin in Auvergne and Languedoc and the Mailletons in Paris.

In 1415, John the Fearless, Duke of Burgundy, signed the Pact of Calais with Henry V of England, by which he acknowledged the King of England and his descendents as heirs to the French throne.

A covenant was signed in Arras on the 2nd of December 1419, by which Philip the Good (John the Fearless's son and the new Duke of Burgundy), acting on behalf of the King of France (Charles VI), decided upon the marriage between Henry V and Catherine of Valois, Charles VI's daughter. From this moment on, it was accepted that the Valois legacy would be passed on to the King of England after the death of his parents-in-law. This covenant was ratified and transformed into a solemn treaty in Troyes where, on the 21st of May 1420, the agreement that was to evict the dauphin was signed, France and England now vowing to be united under the English crown, '*After our death and from that time forward, the crown and kingdom of France, with all their rights and appurtenances, shall be vested permanently in our son, King Henry and his heirs,*' as states article 6 of the treaty.
The dauphin, Charles, found himself in the following situation: officially banished, repudiated by his own parents and evicted from the throne; he consequently took refuge on the opposite banks of the Loire and his partisans dwindled.

France's fate now seemed sealed, when something unexpected happened: at the age of 36 – Henry V of England fell sick and died in Vincennes on the 31st of August 1422. Two months later, on the 21st of October, Charles VI in turn passed away. Upon Charles VI's death, Henry VI – then heir to the English throne, was a 10 month-old baby whom it seemed unfitting to crown king. Two of the child's uncles were appointed as regents: the Duke of Gloucester for England and the Duke of Bedford for France.

France was split in two, in a conflict between the Armagnacs, who were loyal to the dauphin, and the Burgundians, who allied with the English. The dauphin Charles tried to reconquer his kingdom, losing the battles of Cravant in 1423 and Verneuil in 1424 in the process.

Everything was scarce: men, means... Charles took refuge in Bourges. Then strange rumours began to spread. It was said that the town of Gien had seen *'a young girl, commonly called the Maid, on her way to the noble dauphin so as to raise the siege of Orléans and take the noble dauphin to Reims for his anointing.'*

Why Armagnacs and Burgundians?

Charles VI – also known as 'the Mad' – suffered from dementia. France was consequently governed by a regency council. Within this council, two clans fought over power: the Burgundian party, led by John the Fearless, and the Armagnacs whose chief was the Duke Louis I of Orléans. Sensing his power gradually slipping away, John the Fearless had the Duke of Orléans assassinated in Paris in 1407. His murderous act resulted in a genuine civil war between the Armagnacs and the Burgundians. John the Fearless took advantage of the resulting chaos to enter Paris, with support from craftsmen and from academics - among whom Pierre Cauchon, a doctor at the University of Paris - but at the cost of five thousand dead in just one week, many of them noblemen from the Armagnac clan. The University exploited the agitation to prepare administrative reform, known as the Cabochien ordinence (although it had no connection with Caboche). This 159-article text aimed at containing the monarchic power and provided for the shared administration of public funds. In an attempted fight against abuse by royal officers, the institution nevertheless succeeded in reinforcing the powers attributed to the Courts of Accounts and the parliament.

In Montereau-Fault-Yonne, in 1419, twelve years after the death of Louis I, an audience was held between the dauphin Charles and the Duke of Burgundy. The duke – John the Fearless – kneeled before the dauphin and, as he rose, he placed his hand on the pommel of his sword for support. Lord Robert of Loire cried out, *'Dare you place your hand on your sword in the presence of My Lord the Dauphin?'* An exclamation that was but a pretext for Tanneguy du Chastel, a member of the king's house, to attack the duke in the face with an axe. It was at this instant that armed men rushed through the door right next to the dauphin, who was taken aside, and John the Fearless's hand was chopped off, just like the Duke of Orléans before him.

No one on the Burgundian side was surprised, for they knew John the Fearless a ready participant of assassinations and they believed the cries to come from the dauphin and the Armagnacs. The murder had been prepared eighteen days previously, in Montargis, under the impetus of Jean Louvet, President of Provence. He was rewarded by the dauphin, yet dismissed in 1425. Although Charles personally struck no blow, his passiveness during the assassination designated him as its key instigator.

THE BASTILLE OF SAINT-LOUP IS TRULY DAUNTING.
THE FRENCH STRUGGLE.
THE ENGLISH RESIST...
... AND JOAN'S ARMY SUFFERS HEAVY LOSSES.
JOAN, JOAN!
THESE DEVILSOME ENGLISHMEN ARE NOT GIVING UP! WE WILL NEVER TAKE THE FORTRESS!
WE'D BETTER... ARGH!
TCHACK!!!
BACK OFF? NEVER!
MY LOYAL SOLDIERS ARE WITH ME! FOR GOD! FOR FRANCE!
13

GALVANISED BY THE YOUNG WARRIOR, THE FRENCH TROOPS' ARDOUR IS MULTIPLIED...
JOAN LEADS THE ASSAULT...
... TAKING HER MEN, WITH FERVOUR...
... TOWARDS VICTORY!
AND ON THE EVENING OF THE 4TH OF MAY, SAINT-LOUP FALLS.
ON THE 5TH, THE AUGUSTINS BASTILLE IN TURN...
AND NOW...
... LET'S EJECT THOSE DARN ENGLISHMEN FROM THE TOP OF THE TOURELLES!

SIR GLASDALE! THE FRENCH HAVE REACHED THE MOAT!
WHAT?

MIND BLOWING!

THAT DAMNED MAID...
SHE DARED!

JOAN LEADS THE ATTACK ONCE MORE. BUT THIS TIME...

AAAAH!
ZWEECCHACK!!!

SAINT MICHAEL, WHAT ARE YOU DOING?

JOAN!
ARE YOU FORSAKING ME?

I KNEW I WOULD BE WOUNDED...
I PREDICTED IT...
IT'S OVER.
WE ARE GOING TO LOSE HER...
IT'LL TAKE A MIRACLE.

SAINT MICHAEL, DO NOT ABANDON ME, GIVE THEM THEIR MIRACLE...

DO IT FOR THEM...

FOR THE KINGDOM OF FRANCE!

Huile
Miel
AMONG THE ENGLISH RANKS, NEWS SPREADS THAT THE MAID IS BELIEVED DEAD.
THE ENEMY REJOICES, ALREADY REVELLING IN VICTORY...
YET, AGAINST ALL EXPECTATIONS, THAT EVENING...
WHAT? HOLY GOD!

CONVINCED IT WAS INVINCIBLE AND ALREADY VICTORIOUS A FEW HOURS EARLIER, THE ENGLISH ARMY BEGINS TO PANIC...
HOW CAN WE FIGHT AGAINST THIS IMMORTAL, SHE IS GOD'S PROTÉGÉE?!
ON MAY 8TH 1429, ORLÉANS IS FREED...
GLASDALE DIES BY DROWNING.
JOAN HAS KEPT HER PROMISE.

The battles

Joan of Arc only had two years and three months of 'public' life: from 13th February 1429, with her departure from Vaucouleurs, to 23rd May 1430, with her capture in Compiègne, and from 24th May 1430 to 30th May 1431, from her imprisonment to her death, in Rouen.

During her fifteen months of freedom, her days were far from idle. She travelled through a war-stricken land to meet with the king in Chinon; then she headed for Poitiers, before returning to Chinon, all on horseback. Then began a period of battles on no less than eight different sites, of which Orléans is the most famous Yet, let us not forget Jargeau, Patay, Troyes, Saint-Pierre-le-Moûtier and Compiègne, all victorious, whereas before Paris and La Charité-sur-Loire, Joan was forced into retreat. She was seriously wounded in two places: in Orléans, on her left shoulder, then in Paris, on her right thigh; she also suffered a less serious head injury in Jargeau. Yet, let us begin with the Battle of Orléans. It was a traditional battle involving the besieged, the people of Orléans, and the besiegers, the English. The River Loire was in the middle and each side was entrenched, either within the fortified town or in earthen fortresses. Orléans had been under siege for seven months; however, the real encirclement began on the 23rd of October 1428 and food supplies began to cruelly lack. A convoy set off towards Orléans, under the protection of the Marshal, Jean de Brosse, and of Joan of Arc. Joan took up residence with the Duke of Orléans' treasurer and, over several days, she inspected the English bastilles, enjoining them to immediately leave. The English simply burst out laughing, 'wickedly' crying out the worst possible insults.

Joan's anger persisted, as the captains failed to attack. The 4th of May 1429 saw the return of the royal army to Orléans and, that very evening, they collectively launched an attack on the bastille of St Loup. Joan, who had not initially been informed of this attack, cried out, '*Quick, my weapons, my horse!*' and she rushed to the battle site. Her arrival galvanised the French troops who then seized the bastille.

The following day, the 5th of May, was Ascension Day, a day of truce. It was therefore on the 6th of May that Joan, in the company of Étienne de Vignolles, known as La Hire, crossed the Loire over a boat bridge to attack the bastille of St. Jean, which they found abandoned. The English then began to counter-attack from the bastille des Augustins, but Joan and La Hire repelled them, capturing the stronghold. The surviving English troops took refuge in the Tourelles gatehouse.

Joan returned to Orléans for the night and, on the 7th of May, the attack resumed, targeting the Tourelles gatehouse. It was a day of combat, during which Joan was wounded in the shoulder by an arrow. Away from the battlefield, she was tended to with olive oil and pig fat. However, learning that her wounds had disheartened her troops, she resumed fighting. Galvanised by her return, the French followed their heroin to victory. On the 8th of May, the English retreated towards Meung-sur-Loire. The town was wild with joy and, every year since the 8th of May 1429, the people of Orléans have continued to organise a procession in Joan's honour.

The next day, Joan and 'the Bastard' of Orléans set off to meet with the dauphin in Loches. During their parleys, the young warfaring woman suggested he head for Reims to be crowned king. With Joan's help, the Duke of Alençon was charged with clearing the outskirts of Orléans.

Not far from there, in Jargeau, they came across their first hurdle. Upon his arrival, the Duke of Alençon hesitated, he who was not so fond of the dauphin, he who would later betray him twice. He was as pitiful a politician as he was a strategist. Seeking to reassure him, Joan said, *'Gentle duke, do you fear? Do you not know that I have promised your wife I will bring you home safe and sound?'* Joan and the duke were accompanied by three energetic captains - d'Illiers, the bastard of Orléans and La Hire who, upon the council of war, urged for the assault to be immediately launched. Hence, the attack began and it was of such violence that, when the Earl of Suffolk tried to surrender, nobody even heard him.

At the foot of the fortifications, as she was making her way up a ladder, Joan was wounded when a stone struck her helmet. She simply stood up and headed into battle once more. The town was taken a few minutes later and the English surrendered after Suffolk had dubbed Guillaume Regnault, the knight who had taken him prisoner.

Beaugency was in turn delivered without a fight on the 12th of June. The English withdrew to Patay. However, with the French hot on their heels, they decided to hide their archers amidst the hedges that lined the roadway. Yet, they failed to find a suitable hiding place and, preferring to stick with the bulk of the troop, they remounted their horses. A passing deer spurred cries of fright which alerted the French vanguard of their position. They were immediately under attack. It was sheer chaos: Fastolf shot off at a gallop to rally round the fleeing troops. The men were on the outskirts of Patay and, as they saw their chief approach at lightning speed, they presumed he was fleeing and, in turn, took flight. It is said that two thousand English soldiers were killed and two hundred taken prisoner, for only three losses on the French side.

The road to the crown was now open; the future king regained confidence and decided to launch a major attack towards Reims. He was counting on the moral impact of his victory in Patay, so that the other towns that paved his way would also surrender. His troops finally reached Reims, where the dauphin was crowned King Charles VII.

17TH JULY 1429...
REIMS...
DONG
DONG
DONG
DONG
DONG
I CAN HARDLY BELIEVE IT, JOAN...

HERE WE ARE, REUNITED...

... TO ATTEND CHARLES' ANOINTING...

CONVINCING THE GOOD KING TO LEAVE LOCHES WAS, INDEED, A DIFFICULT TASK.

... AND CONVINCING YOU TO HEAD FOR REIMS RATHER THAN ATTACKING NORMANDY!

HERE, A MIRACLE IS UPON US...

AND IT IS BY THE GRACE OF GOD THAT WE ARE ALL HERE TODAY!

THIS 17TH OF JULY 1429 WILL GO DOWN IN HISTORY...
CHARLES IS ANOINTED WITH THE OIL FROM THE HOLY AMPULLA. HE IS KING AT LAST.
THE KINGDOM HAS FOUND ITS LEADER...
AND IT PLEASES GOD!
LONG LIVE THE KING!
LONG LIVE THE KING!
LONG LIVE THE KING!
LONG LIVE CHARLES VII!
20

MEANWHILE, IN REIMS, THE KING'S SUPPORTERS REJOICE...

COULD GOD AND THE DEVIL BE DOING BATTLE IN SECRET?
ONE NEVER KNOWS...
ONE THING IS SURE: CHARLES VII'S TROOPS RELIEVE THE ENGLISH OF THE TOWN OF LAON, COMPIEGNE AND BEAUVAIS.

BUT IN PARIS...
THE CITY REMAINS IMPENETRABLE...

AND JOAN IS WOUNDED ONCE MORE.
THE KING IS PLANNING A TRUCE WITH THE DUKE OF BURGUNDY AND THE ENGLISH...

FROM NOW ON, THINGS WILL CHANGE FOR YOUNG JOAN...
A TRUCE? AFTER ALL WE'VE ACHIEVED?

YES, JOAN, THE ARMY HAS BEEN DISSOLVED...

BUT THE KING IS NOT AN UNGRATEFUL MAN...

HE THANKS YOU FOR YOUR LOYAL SERVICES AND TO DEMONSTRATE HIS GRATITUDE...

... HE ENNOBLES YOU ALONG WITH ALL THE MEMBERS OF YOUR FAMILY.

STOP FIGHTING, JOAN...
CHARLES IS KING... YOU HAVE FULFILLED YOUR MISSION!

A LONG AND COLD WINTER ENFOLDS THE COUNTRYSIDE AND JOAN IS OFFERED A MOMENT'S RESPITE...
23

BUT AS SOON AS SPRING ARRIVES...

WITH NO GENUINE SUPPORT FROM THE KING, JOAN TAKES UP WEAPONS AGAIN.
THE FELON PHILIP THE GOOD HAS BESIEGED COMPIEGNE.

WE MUST GO AND FREE THE TOWN!

WITH HER TROOPS, THE MAID OF ORLEANS HEADS FOR COMPIEGNE.

BUT, AT THE CITY GATES, WHEN JOAN DARES TO VENTURE OUTDOORS...
THE MAID, BRING HER DOWN!
JOAN FALLS OFF HER HORSE...
... AND IS TAKEN PRISONER!

CORONATION AND DISILLUSION

In Châlons-en-Champagne, on the road to the coronation in Reims, Joan of Arc met with a number of inhabitants from Domremy and Vaucouleurs, who had come here upon the future king's invitation. The dauphin Charles received a delegation of burghers from Reims at the Château de Sept-Saulx. They vowed to him their full and total obedience. On the evening of the 16th of July 1429, he entered the city in the heart of Champagne, a province that was largely under Burgundian control.

The coronation ceremony began the following day. It was far from a simple affair for the coronation adornments were in Saint-Denis, in the hands of the English; however, the most important of them all – the ampulla containing the holy oil - was there, in Reims.

Some of the kingdom's 'peers*' were also absent due to civil war. Hence, the Duke of Bedford, the regent of the duchies of Normandy and Guyenne, could not attend and swear his allegiance to the king. The peers who were unable to attend the coronation were replaced by other noblemen whom the king wished to honour but could not pay. At the time, missing the coronation was considered as treason.

Twelve peers were present, six laymen and six clergymen. They had a role to play during the ceremony and were entrusted with royal attributes: a tunic adorned with the fleur-de-lis, cope, crown, sceptre, hand of justice, belt, gold spurs, sword and ring. Joan stood next to the king, brandishing her standard for, *'he had been much pained and it was rightful that he be honoured.'* On her armour, she wore, *'highly noble attire of draped gold and rich silk...'* It was with great surprise that the most noble people of the kingdom saw her in such posture. Joan's parents, and all the inhabitants of Domremy, rejoiced and Jack d'Arc readily forgave his daughter for leaving home without his consent.

Joan waited for the princes to pay homage to King Charles VII before coming before him to kneel and say, *'Gentle king, here, God's will has been executed... He has shown that you are a true king.'*

* Title awarded during the Middle Ages to the king's leading vassals.

Joan observed, and confided in the archbishop of Reims, *'I would like to put down my weapons and go and serve my father and my mother.'* She had only accomplished part of what the voices had asked her: to have the dauphin crowned king; she was yet to deliver the kingdom of France. Victim to her own duty, she set up her troops in Saint-Denis under the Duke of Alençon's command. Inside the basilica, Joan placed the pieces of her freshly broken sword as she chased away the prostitutes that were pursuing her army.

The following day, the king left Reims to head for the priory in Corbeny where he 'cared for' the sick suffering from scrofula. According to legend, this serious skin condition (which causes purulent fistulae) could be cured by certain saints and kings of France and England. Hence, Charles VII satisfied one of the three traditions that, following 14th century custom, completed the coronation ceremony. The two other traditions were more difficult to abide by, given the political state of affairs at the time: he was to hold his first court in the abbey of St. Denis and to make a solemn entry into Paris, at the time an Anglo-Burgundian territory. To do so, he needed to take up arms and deliver Paris.

In a fit of anger, the Duke of Bedford admonished his fleeing war chiefs and the *'numerous deserters that the terror caused by the magical incantations of the Maid had set fleeing to their homeland.'*

Joan wrote a letter to the Duke of Burgundy, inviting him to join the king. However, Philip the Good replied by proposing a truce, which Charles VII hurried to accept.

The king's army headed towards Paris, without encountering any genuine confrontation. Late August, Senlis was taken and the Duke of Bedford left Paris to organise the defence of Normandy, leaving Paris in the hands of Lewis of Luxembourg, the bishop of Thérouanne.

On the 16th of August, Charles left for Crépy, then Compiègne. The English offered the king a four-month truce, which he accepted.

Paris was protected by a double ditch. A first dry ditch (four to six metres deep and eight to fifteen metres wide), an earthen embankment of around ten metres and standing two metres above ground level, then a second ditch, in the form of a moat and, finally the city walls. Orléans had only been protected by a single ditch and a wall. The siege had lasted eight months, with no result.

It was essential that the besieged come out and wage battle; however, the Parisians remained within their city walls, despite continuous provocation. After fourteen days, Joan ordered for the assault to be launched, yet it yielded no result. A second attempt was made on the 8th of September 1429; this time, Joan was hit in the thigh with an arrow and one of her pages was killed when an arrow struck his eye.

Through René d'Anjou, the king ordered for the attack - which he deemed doomed to failure - to be abandoned and for troops to withdraw to the Loire. The royal army raised the siege and headed for Gien. Joan, who was wounded, was 'begged' to seek medical attention and to take rest for a few days in Bourges, with the king's general councillor of finance. Then Charles VII called upon her once more, most probably to test her, asking her to get rid of Perrinet Gressart, a fearsome bandit. She reconquered Saint-Pierre-le-Moûtier; however, in La Charité-sur-Loire, she failed. Winter was approaching and she withdrew to the Loire.

THE CASTLE IN BEAULIEU-EN-VERMANDOIS...
OCTOBER 1430.

JOAN IS IN THE HANDS OF JOHN OF LUXEMBOURG, A SINISTER CHARACTER...

YOU ARE PENSIVE, MY MAID... WHAT TROUBLES YOU?

YOUR EVIL DEALINGS, WHERE DO YOU STAND WITH YOUR NEGOTIATIONS?

I AM RAISING THE STAKES...

25

THE ENGLISH ARE SHOWING GREAT INTEREST, THEY ARE CELEBRATING YOUR CAPTURE... AND THEY ARE WILLING TO PAY DEARLY FOR YOUR SKIN...

... AND TO SEE YOU AT THE STAKE!

YOUR LUNCH, YOUNG GIRL...
THANK YOU, LEAVE IT ON THE TABLE, YOUR LORD HAS SPOILT MY APPETITE!

COME ON, BE REASONABLE. YOU MUST EAT TO...

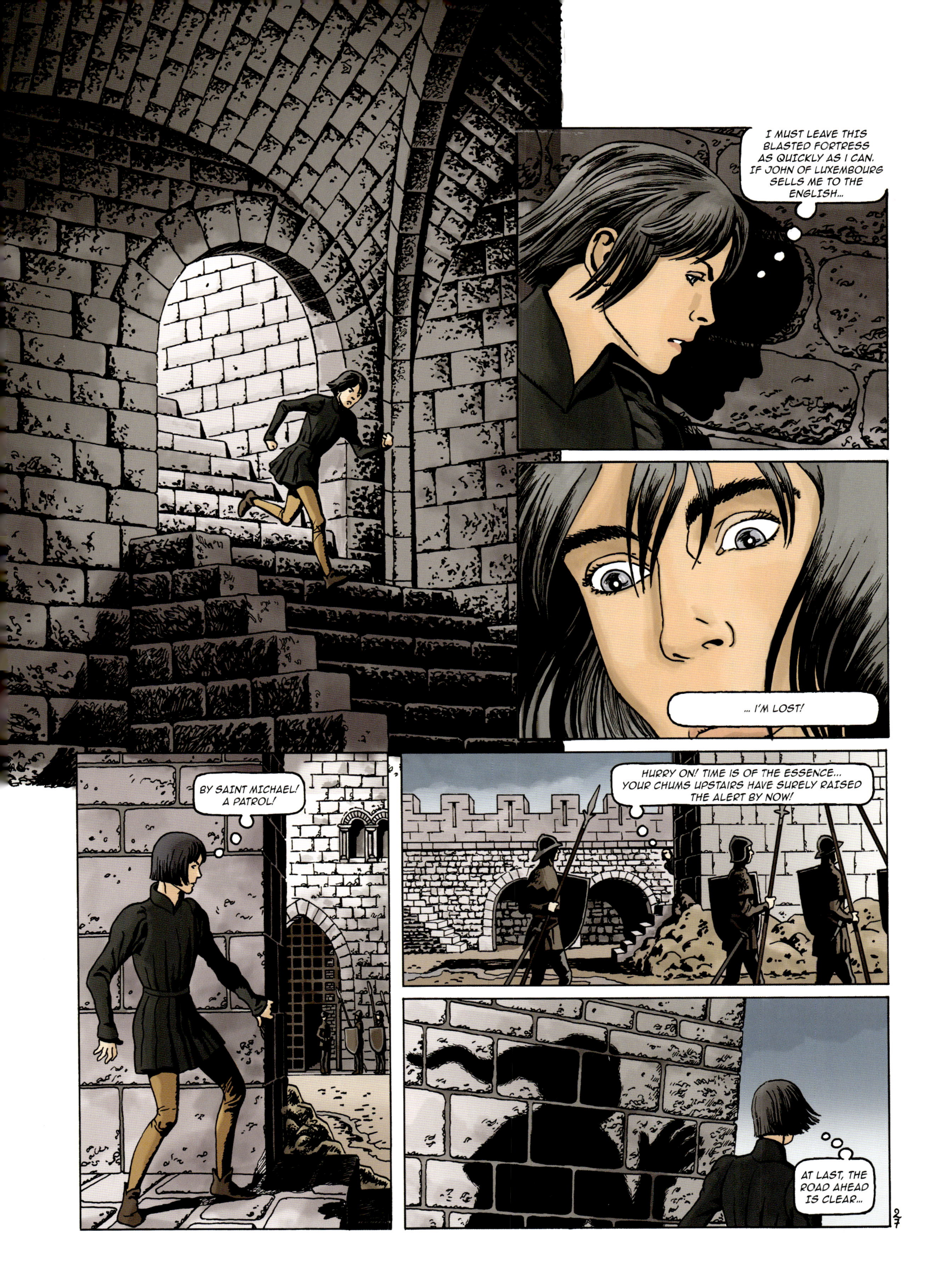
I MUST LEAVE THIS BLASTED FORTRESS AS QUICKLY AS I CAN. IF JOHN OF LUXEMBOURG SELLS ME TO THE ENGLISH...
... I'M LOST!
BY SAINT MICHAEL! A PATROL!
HURRY ON! TIME IS OF THE ESSENCE... YOUR CHUMS UPSTAIRS HAVE SURELY RAISED THE ALERT BY NOW!
AT LAST, THE ROAD AHEAD IS CLEAR...
27

AHA! SO WHERE DO YOU THINK YOU'RE GOING SWEETHEART?
?!
THIS WILL AMUSE OUR LORD...
LET ME GO, YOU DIRTY ANIMAL!
MASTER, LOOK WHAT I HAVE FOUND!
YOU'RE HURTING ME!!
WELL, WELL, THE MAID...
SO YOU WANTED TO ESCAPE? YOU'VE HAD ENOUGH OF BEAULIEU-EN-VERMANDOIS... UNDERSTANDABLE.
I WILL NOW SHOW YOU THE WALLS OF BEAUREVOIR...

MY VOICES... GIVE ME THE STRENGTH TO ESCAPE... TO ESCAPE OR TO DIE!

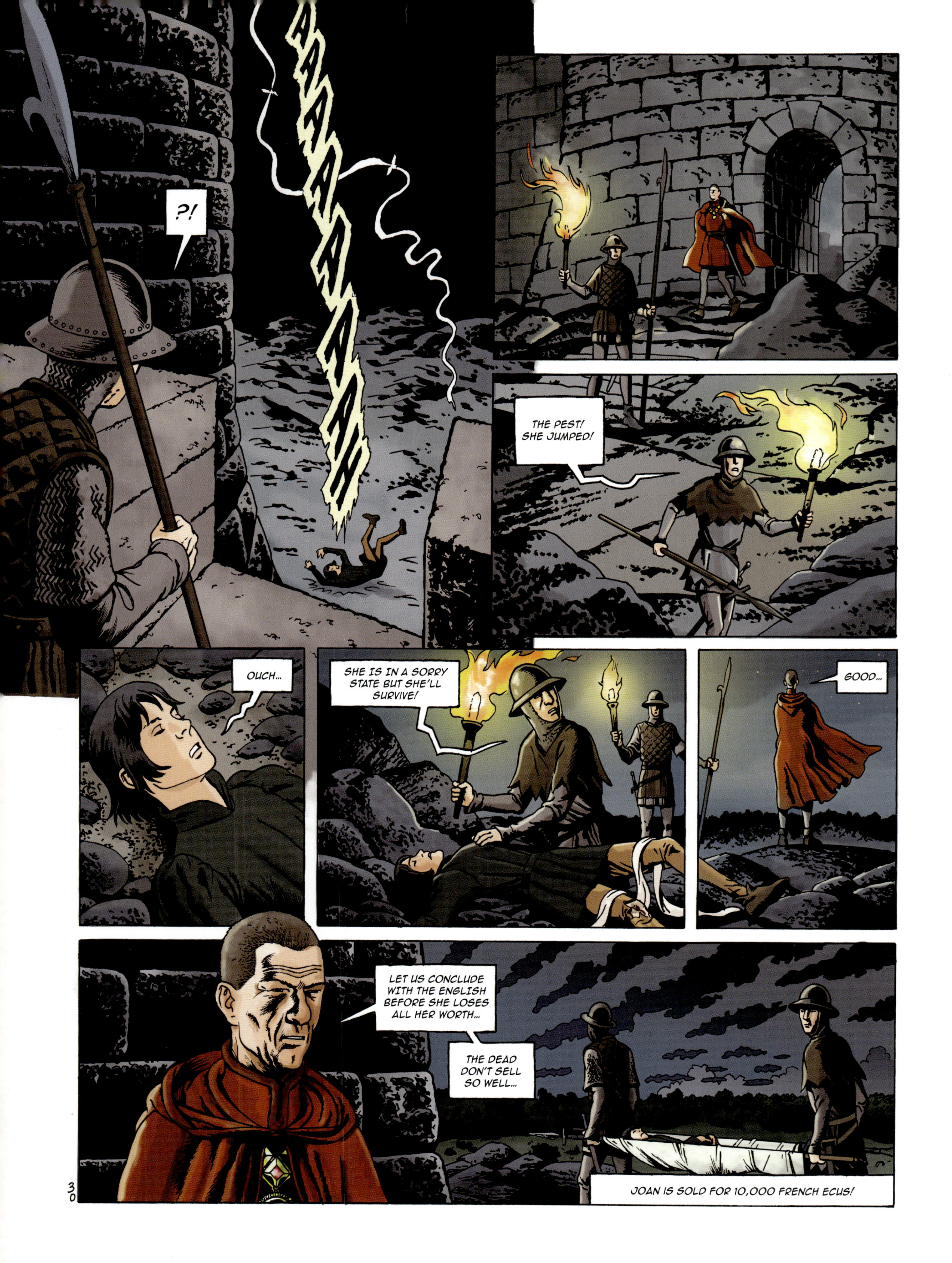
?!
AAAAAAAAAAH
THE PEST! SHE JUMPED!
OUCH...
SHE IS IN A SORRY STATE BUT SHE'LL SURVIVE!
GOOD...
LET US CONCLUDE WITH THE ENGLISH BEFORE SHE LOSES ALL HER WORTH...
THE DEAD DON'T SELL SO WELL...
JOAN IS SOLD FOR 10,000 FRENCH ECUS!
30

THE END OF AN EPIC

Over the winter of 1429-1430, Charles VII ennobled Joan's family. He was concerned that negotiations with the Anglo-Burgundians were yielding no ground. In April, the English had reinforcements land in Calais. Joan, in the company of her brother Peter and Poton de Xaintrailles, decided to set off with troops to help her *'good friends from Compiègne'.*

Compiègne was a stopper on the River Oise that prevented any liaison between the Burgundian lands and those of the English. King Charles VII had considered conceding it to the Duke of Burgundy during negotiations over the suspension of hostilities on the 28th of August 1429. However, the inhabitants were against any such concession, preferring to remain loyal to the King of France. The forces engaged were unbalanced, the Anglo-Burgundians boasting around 3,600 men, whereas the town only had 390 men-at-arms and 210 bowmen (archers and crossbowmen). Thankfully, the River Oise and its fortifications rendered the position easy to defend.

Joan arrived on the 23rd of May 1430 and secretly entered the town. That afternoon, she decided to head for Margny-lès-Compiègne, located to the north of the River Oise, to launch an offensive against the Burgundians. Around five to six hundred men travelled with her to attack some 2,670 Burgundian combatants. However, their initiative did not quite go according to plan. Fearing for their lives, Joan of Arc's men withdrew towards the St. Louis bridge over the river. Having seen the attack from the north, the English set off in pursuit of the fleeing French troops. Joan found herself to the rear, with the Burgundians following fast behind. The captain of the town, William of Flavy, took fright before this surge of assailants and he closed the bridge portcullis.

Joan and the French troops were now trapped between the closed gate and the Anglo-Burgundians. Joan, her brother Peter, her squire Jean d'Aulon and Poton de Xaintrailles were all taken prisoner. She was immediately brought before Philip the Good. *'We must beware of this inclination to find a great guilty party for every great catastrophe,'* the historian and politician, Henri Wallon, was later to say. The Sire of Flacy was responsible for his town and was faced with a difficult choice: to save Joan and, in the process, perhaps enable the English to invade the city, or to lower the bridge portcullis and save his town. Joan never begrudged his choice for she knew, and had even said, that she would be captured within the year. Today, his choice is considered simply as an unfortunate decision for the Maid.

Hence, Joan was in the hands of the Burgundians rather than the English. This made no real difference for the Duke of Burgundy was a vassal to both the King of France and the King of England.

And a vassal must hand over any important prisoner to his suzerain in exchange for a reward. She was therefore handed over to the Duke of Bedford and the amount of the reward was set.

Joan was transferred to the castle in Beaulieu-en-Vermandois on the 26th of May. Jean d'Aulon stayed with her throughout her imprisonment. Despite accusations of heresy proclaimed by the University of Paris, she was allowed to leave the jail to go and pray in the castle chapel. Her cell was on the first floor of one of the enclosure towers. In May, she succeeded in locking her gaolers inside her cell; however, as she fled, she was arrested by the porter. Henceforth, she was kept under lock and key in a small dark room and was no longer afforded such liberty. On the 7th of June she was brought before the Duke and the Duchess of Burgundy upon the latter's request. The duchess and her daughter offered Joan women's clothing, which she refused since she had received no such orders from God.

Learning of the Maid's attempted escape, John of Luxembourg decided to have her transferred to the castle in Beaurevoir, a powerful fortress belonging to his family. It was customary for prisoners to give their word not to escape; however, no mention is made of any such promise in her trial proceedings. Joan also tried to escape from Beaurevoir, stipulating that in no way did she wish to die, but, on the contrary, to escape from the tower in order to return to combat and *'to go and help many good people who were in need.'* This time, she tried to escape by means of a makeshift rope which she had produced by pleating her bed sheets and covers. However, the resulting 'rope' was too short, or not strong enough, and Joan fell into the ditch that surrounded the castle. The guards found her in a pitiful state and she was tended to.

On the 21st of November 1430, Joan of Arc was transferred to Arras to be handed over to the English in exchange for ten thousand crowns. Then began a long journey towards Rouen, where she was to be judged. She discovered the sea in Crotoy and Saint-Valéry-sur-Somme. Then the convoy headed for Rouen, avoiding any zones within which someone may have sought to free her. On the 23rd of December, the day before Christmas Eve, she was locked up in the castle tower in Rouen, *'overlooking the fields'*. Three men of war kept an eye on her and her feet were clapped in irons.

As a prisoner, her active life was now over, but her mission continued. Without her captivity, we would never have known her great fighting spirit. Without her trial, we would still have seen her as the young 'shepherdess'. By seeking to condemn her, the English revealed her great intelligence before the insidious questions of those appointed to judge her and, above all, they paved the way for a monument in her memory.

ROUEN...
CHRISTMAS 1430...
AHHH! HERE SHE IS AT LAST!!!
I'VE BEEN WAITING FOR THIS FOR NEARLY SIX MONTHS!
COME DOWN FROM YOUR HORSE, MAID.
I TRUST YOUR STAY WITH THE BURGUNDIANS WAS NOT TOO... UNPLEASANT.
THEY SEEMED VERY KEEN ON YOU... 10,000 ECUS IS QUITE A SUM!
I HAD TO NEGOTIATE!
BUT IN THE END, EVERYONE GIVES IN TO PIERRE CAUCHON...
WHETHER A BURGUNDIAN, A MAID OR... A WITCH!
31

DID YOU KNOW I HAVE BEEN APPOINTED BY THE ENGLISH AUTHORITIES?
ON THEIR BEHALF, I WILL BE IN CHARGE OF YOUR TRIAL!

A TRIAL OVERSEEN BY THE ENGLISH?!! DO YOU THINK MY KING WILL TOLERATE SUCH AN INSULT?
I FOUGHT FOR HIM!

OF COURSE, JOAN...
NO ONE IS QUESTIONING YOUR MILITARY FEATS...
YOU WILL BE JUDGED FOR HERESY!

TAKE HER TO HER DUNGEON AND KEEP AN EYE ON HER!

AT LEAST UNTIL SHE IS JUDGED FOR WITCHCRAFT!

AM I SUCH A GREAT THREAT THAT YOU MUST KEEP ME SHACKLED SO? AND... STOP LOOKING AT ME LIKE THAT!

IT'S CAUCHON WHO WANTS YOU TO BE TREATED SO WELL!
AND IT'S A CHARMING SIGHT, WHAT A PLEASURE IT IS TO FOLLOW ORDERS! HEHEHE!

YOU ARE HOGS!

THESE DAYS IT'S NOT SO MUCH THE HOGS THAT END UP ON THE SPIT!
HAHAHA!

WITCH!

I SHOULD BE IN A CHURCH PRISON, SINCE MY CRIME IS A RELIGIOUS ONE!
THE COURT OF INQUISITION HAS DECIDED OTHERWISE...

I DO NOT GIVE MUCH FOR YOUR CHANCES!

MONTSIGNOR, EITHER YOUR PRIESTS MAKE THIS SHE-DEVIL REPENT FOR ALL HER SINS, OR I WILL TAKE HER BACK...

WE WILL CONDUCT A TRIAL THAT WILL GO DOWN IN HISTORY, BEDFORD!

DAMN! I WANT THAT GIRL BURNT, ONCE AND FOR ALL!

TWO WEEKS LATER...
MY VOICES, WHY HAS THE KING DONE NOTHING FOR ME?

WHY WAIT...
I CALL THIS MARTYRDOM...

I KNOW NOT WHETHER I CAN ENDURE MORE SUFFERING...

I...
I SUBMIT MYSELF TO OUR LORD...

KLANK
?!

STAND UP MAID, YOUR TIME HAS COME!
35

ON THE MORNING OF THE 9TH OF JANUARY 1431...
A CHAPEL... LET ME PRAY JUST A MOMENT...
FORWARD!
JUST A MOMENT!
YOU...YOU HAVE NO RIGHT!
LET ME PRAY...
ENTER!
GOOD MORNING, JOAN...
COME CLOSER...
INTRODUCE YOURSELF TO YOUR JUDGES...

Pierre Cauchon

My name is Pierre Cauchon and I was born around the year 1371 in Reims. I belonged to a family of modest middle-class notables. I became a master of art at the age of 20, before studying canon law and theology. My studies took me to Paris, far from my birthplace. My peers were quick to acknowledge me: at the age of 20, I was honoured with a position of school dean and, at 26, rector for a period of two years. As a rector, I had judicial powers over university affairs and students, who did not fall under the authority of the king's police. Perhaps I developed a taste for such power. This would at least explain my conviction that I was always right and my aversion to contradiction. As a man of arms, yet not a nobleman, I would have had to content myself with a subordinate role, hence my early decision to opt for the Church, which offered me better prospects. I served as a priest in Sens, yet I never lived there. I only did so for the money.

My employment at the University of Paris and the various positions I occupied gained me renown and I was sent on a mission to meet with the Pope of Avignon and the Pope of Rome. However, following the example of other ecclesiastics, I realised that it was only by obtaining the favours of a prince or a man of power that I could accede to a prestigious career.

King Charles VI was in such a state of madness that the kingdom was forced to choose two regents: the king's uncle John, Duke of Berry and his brother Louis of Orléans. The Queen Isabeau of Bavaria and the court were the subject of violent reprimands on the part of the University. There was no choice but to resort to the Duke of Burgundy, John the Fearless. It was a good choice and I became Archdeacon of Chartres and of Châlons-en-Champagne, Canon of Reims and of Beauvais, chaplain for the Duke of Burgundy and auditor for the Pope, the accumulated income of which brought me around two thousand livres per year. During a mission to the Council of Constance, I attended the trial of a Czech theologian accused of heresy. His name was John Hus and he was burned at the stake in 1415. This instructive experience was to serve me later.

Alas, on the 10th of September 1419, my protector was assassinated by the Armagnacs. I then decided to offer my services to the Duke of Normandy (or should I say the English). A treaty between King Charles VI of France and King Henry V of England was concluded in Troyes – a treaty drafted, under my initiative, by my niece's husband. My contribution to the said treaty offered me exposure among illustrious figures, upon whose recommendation, the Pope appointed me Bishop of Beauvais. This appointment distanced me from Burgundy, whilst bringing me closer to the English party. Henry V of England had me enter the king's council and I was in charge of winning over certain towns to the Anglo-Burgundian cause. Alas, my popularity was at an all time low: at the time, I was in charge of collecting a number of charges and taxes in Champagne and in Normandy. Since the Treaty of Troyes in 1420, the people could not quite understand my continued loyalty towards the decision to choose Henry V as Charles VI's successor. Yet, up to my very last breath, I remained faithful to this choice that had brought me such glory – I, a mediocre burgher from Troyes. I could no longer stay in my lovely town of Beauvais, for the inhabitants had decided to side with the new King Charles VII. I therefore packed my bags and headed for Rouen, the capital of Normandy, where I took refuge. At the time, the position of archbishop for the town was vacant. I took up residence in the Hôtel de Lisieux, located near the Church of Saint-Candé. There, on several occasions, I welcomed the cathedral canons and dignitaries. However, the Bishop of Thérouanne, Louis of Luxembourg, had earned support from the chapter and the Pope himself, and it was upon the Duke of Burgundy's influence that Hugh V des Orges was appointed. You who read me now, you know of me as the leading judge in the Maid of Orleans' trial, but also by my name, which many scoffed at: the name Cauchon is in fact derived from Normandy or Picardy dialect and means slipper ('chausson' in French). It therefore bears no connection whatsoever to the word pig ('cochon' in French).

Joan was captured in Compiègne, beyond the River Oise, therefore under the jurisdiction of Beauvais. Had she been captured before the river, the bishopric of Soissons would been the competent territory. As Bishop of Beauvais, it was perfectly normal for me to be in charge of the trial, my principal aim being to make it an exemplary trial that would eradicate any last memory of this 'maid' – down to her very name. I could well have decided to subject her to the judgment of God, through a trial by ordeal; however, since the English considered her to be a witch, I decided to try her for heresy. I took great care to surround myself with men who were capable of sitting on such a court of inquisition. A total of 133 judges and assessors (eight of whom were English) were chosen. As a judge, I was but the authorised representative of the English power. The English king's two uncles, Bedford and Winchester, kept a watchful eye on me and the trial was held within the walls of Rouen Castle. It was a long and painstaking trial, the outcome of which is known to all.

Seven months after the sentence was executed, I was appointed within the organisation in charge of Normandy's finances and, as a Peer of France, I attended the coronation of King Henry VI in Paris. Afterwards, my life was a matter of missions and conferences. Exhausted, I finally contented myself with arbitrating ecclesiastical problems in Rouen, where I had taken up permanent residence.

Pierre Cauchon died suddenly in 1442 at the age of 71, whilst at his barber's in Rouen.

21ST FEBRUARY 1431, THE PRELATES ARE FACING JOAN...
... FACING HISTORY.
MONSIGNOR, I WISH TO CONFESS...
OUT OF THE QUESTION. UNLESS YOU TELL US THE TRUTH...

DO YOU SWEAR TO TELL THE WHOLE THE TRUTH?
I WILL TELL YOU...

BUT I WON'T SAY IT ALL.
BEWARE OF WHAT YOU DO! I HAVE BEEN SENT BY GOD: YOU ARE EXPOSING YOURSELVES TO GREAT DANGER!

CAN YOU HEAR THIS HERETIC THREATENING US?!
NO!
IS THIS NOT PROOF ENOUGH THAT WE FACE A WITCH?...

SENT BY THE DEVIL!...
JOAN...
DO YOU KNOW IF YOU ARE IN THE GRACE OF GOD?

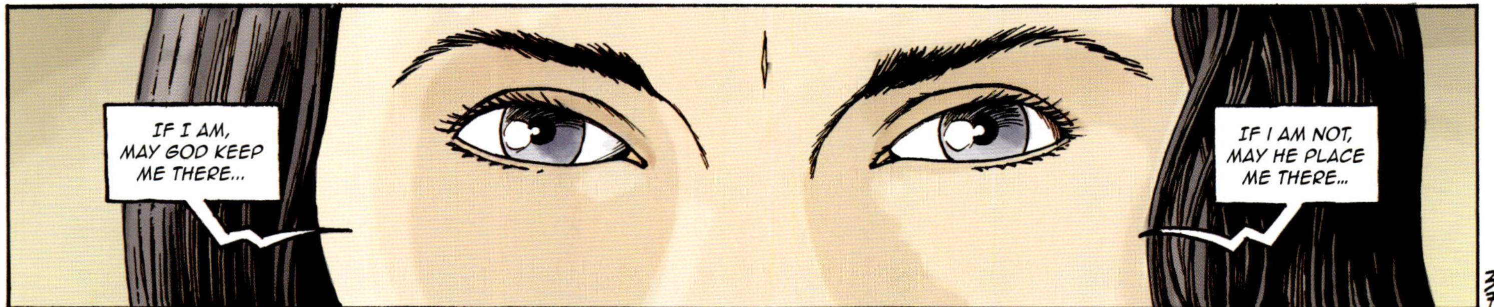
IF I AM, MAY GOD KEEP ME THERE...
IF I AM NOT, MAY HE PLACE ME THERE...

THE GIRL IS SHREWD, MONSIGNOR...

JOAN, YOU WHO KNOW SO MUCH, CAN YOU TELL ME: DOES GOD HATE THE ENGLISH?

OF THE LOVE OR THE HATRED GOD HAS FOR THE ENGLISH AND OF WHAT HE DOES WITH THEIR SOULS, I KNOW NOTHING...

BUT I DO KNOW THAT THEY WILL BE CHASED OUT OF FRANCE, EXCEPT THOSE WHO DIE HERE...
... AND GOD WILL OFFER THE FRENCH VICTORY OVER THE ENGLISH!
AND DO YOU BELIEVE YOU HAVE DONE GOOD IN DONNING A MAN'S CLOTHES?
EVERYTHING I HAVE DONE, I HAVE DONE UPON GOD'S WILL AND I BELIEVE I HAVE DONE IT WELL. MAY HE OFFER ME GOOD GUIDANCE AND SUPPORT.

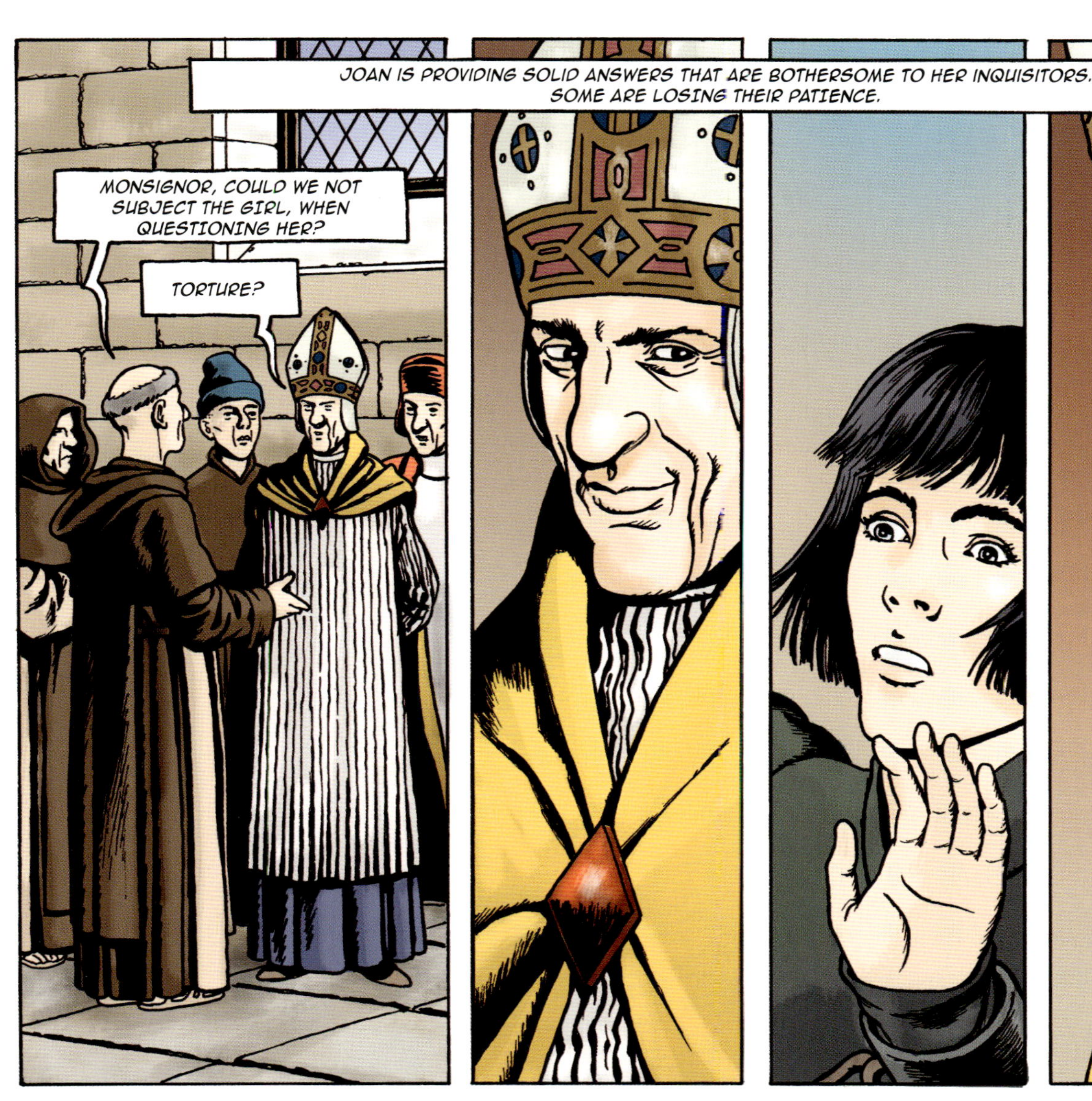
JOAN IS PROVIDING SOLID ANSWERS THAT ARE BOTHERSOME TO HER INQUISITORS. SOME ARE LOSING THEIR PATIENCE.
MONSIGNOR, COULD WE NOT SUBJECT THE GIRL, WHEN QUESTIONING HER?
TORTURE?

NO...
IT'S TOO SOON... LET US WAIT...
I AM SURE THAT JOAN WILL DECIDE TO BE REASONABLE...

WON'T YOU JOAN - BE SENSIBLE AND SUBMIT YOURSELF TO THE CHURCH...
NEVER! NEVER WILL I BETRAY MY VOICES!
OH YES YOU WILL, MY YOUNG MAID... JUST WAIT AND SEE!

39

ABANDONED BY CHARLES VII...
... ALONE, THE YOUNG WOMAN FACES HER JUDGES, WHO, EVERY DAY, UNVEIL A LITTLE MORE...
... OF THEIR SINISTER SOULS.
FOR FIVE LONG MONTHS, JOAN RETURNS EVERY EVENING TO HER DUNGEON, INSIDE THAT TERRIBLE TOWER...
SHE IS ONLY ALLOWED TO LEAVE FOR INTERMINABLE QUESTIONING...
... SUBJECTED TO HUNGER AND DESPERATION...
... AND ILLNESS.

ON THE 23RD OF MAY 1431...
AS THE PALE DAWN IS RISING...
... IN THE CEMETERY
OF SAINT OUEN IN ROUEN...
A SAD SCENE
IS UNFOLDING...
REPENT YOURSELF OF YOUR SINS BEFORE IT IS TOO LATE! REPENT YOURSELF OF WEARING A MAN'S CLOTHES AND OF DISOBEYING THE CHURCH.
THE STAKE IS READY AND WAITING.
IS THIS WHAT YOU WANT?
SAVE YOURSELF: SUBMIT YOURSELF!
I...
I SUBMIT.

HOWEVER, THREE DAYS LATER, A SCANDALOUS RUMOUR SPREADS THROUGHOUT ROUEN...
JOAN HAS TAKEN TO DRESSING LIKE A MAN AGAIN!

INDEED...
...

BUT HOW DID SHE FIND THESE CLOTHES?
BE QUIET, MARGUERIE, BY THE DEVIL HIMSELF, THIS WITCH IS SURELY ENDOWED WITH POWERS!

WHY DO YOU DON SUCH ATTIRE? HAVE YOU GONE MAD?!
I... I TOOK THEM OF MY OWN WILL. NO ONE HAS FORCED ME!
IT IS MORE FITTING TO DRESS LIKE A MAN AMIDST ALL THESE MEN, THAN TO DRESS LIKE A WOMAN!

YOU PROMISED ME A CHURCH PRISON
WHERE I CAN CONFESS AND PRAY...

IN EXCHANGE, I WILL BE GOOD AND I WILL DO AS IT PLEASES THE CHURCH.
BUT HERE I AM...

... ALONE IN THIS PRISON FULL OF MEN...
I WOULD RATHER DIE THAN BE SHACKLED!

AND YOUR VOICES, WHAT DO YOUR VOICES SAY?!

MY VOICES TOLD ME THAT I WAS WRONG TO CONFESS FOR HAVING FAILED TO CORRECTLY ACCOMPLISH MY DEEDS... BUT GOD HAS FORGIVEN ME. AND ALL THAT I SAID, I SAID SO FOR FEAR OF THE FIRE.
BUT TODAY, I FEAR NO MORE.

DO YOU REALISE THAT YOUR ACTS PROVE YOU HAVE RELAPSED. YOU ARE CONDEMNED!

MY LIFE ENDS HERE...

BUT HISTORY
IS JUST
BEGINNING...

BISHOP,
I DIE BY
YOUR HAND!
!!!

WHATEVER I HAVE
DONE, BE IT RIGHT
OR WRONG...
... IS NOT OF THE KING'S DOING!
AND HIS KINGDOM IS SAFE...

Joan's trial

The trial began on the 9th of January 1431, to end on the 24th of May. We cannot therefore consider it as a hurried one. We must bear in mind that this was a religious trial, consequently based on canon law, which is different from civil law. Joan was threatened with torture, but was never subjected to it. The conditions of detention for female prisoners were not abided by and the trial proceedings were but a summary of the questions put forward to the accused. We have knowledge of answers provided by Joan to questions already asked yet not mentioned in official texts. The notaries and clerks in charge of taking notes did so with a quill and ink. Their notes were then transcribed into French, before being translated into Latin. By this, we mean that her trial was not falsified.

Refusing to participate, or attempting to counter any decisions made by Pierre Cauchon was not devoid of risk. Maître Jean Lohier, a notable Norman clerk, Maître Jean de Lafontaine and Maître Nicolas de Houppeville failed to please the judges and were sent into exile to ensure they did not reappear during the trial. Let us consider the witness report by William Manchon on the subject of Jean de Châtillon, *'During Joan's interrogation, he appeared favourable, stating that she could not be required to answer questions that were... too difficult. His criticism, the terms of which now escape me, did not please the other assessors. They told him several times to leave them to rest. "Yet, I must," retorted Jean de Châtillon, "follow my conscience." Upon which, much ado. The bishop then said to Jean de Châtillon, "Be quiet and leave the judges to speak."'* He was later given notice not to attend any further sessions without being summoned. Certain participants were loyal. For example, during one session, brother Isambard spoke to Joan, trying to guide her, touching on her submission to the Church, *'Be quiet, in the name of the devil,'* the bishop cried to him. Pierre Cauchon and the English representative, the Earl of Warwick, had even introduced a rather repugnant character, Nicolas Loiseleur. He pretended to be one of Joan's compatriots, imprisoned on a different floor of the tower. Then, as a man of the church, he had her confess to him. In general, she was never brought before the judges before the said Loiseleur had conferred with her. Joan was not allowed to confess to any other than him. Hence, she was spied upon by day, by this alleged compatriot, and by night under the surveillance of guards. Yet the trial unfolded in a manner that surprised the judges. These men, so cultivated and accustomed to dealing with complex theological problems expected to very quickly bring the young illiterate peasant to provide confused responses, making her utter words that could then be held against her. However, they found themselves before a young girl who had no intention of being tricked, standing up to them and providing, on the contrary, extremely clear and shrewd answers to their questions.

Pierre warned her that should she escape, she would be sentenced for heresy, to which she replied that a prisoner can escape without necessarily being a heretic. To the question, *'Do you know if you are in the grace of God?'* she replied, *'If I am, may God keep me there and if I am not, may he place me there.'* One of the clerks later said, *'Those who listened to her were stupefied.'* On the subject of her sword, she declared, *'My sword has never killed anyone... I carried the banner when we went to attack.'*
And to, *'Was St. Michael naked when he appeared to you?'* she retorted, *'Do you think God cannot clothe him?'*
As the trial continued, it appeared increasingly evident that it would be difficult, if not impossible, to accuse her of heresy. Yet the charges against her were abundant. She could be accused of having worn men's clothes, by making specific reference to a passage from the Bible. The judges decided that it was a sin to attempt to deceive on the subject of the sex God gives to each and every one. Lame grounds that Cauchon was to nevertheless seize as a sign of disobedience to the laws of the Church.

In any trial for heresy, the penitent can publicly admit to any wrongs committed and return to the Church: this act is referred to as abjuration. On the 24th of May 1431, in the Saint-Ouen cemetery, Joan acknowledged her offence and signed her confession by means of a cross, despite the fact that she was perfectly capable of signing her name. She then asked to be taken to a Church prison and to be guarded by women. Although she was given a dress, contrary to his judges' commitments, Pierre Cauchon ordered for her to be taken back to where she had come from, in other words to Rouen Castle. Two days later, Joan once more donned her masculine attire, the only clothes in which she felt safe amidst all these men.
Pierre Cauchon hurried forth, convinced that his ruse had succeeded. She told him, *'All that I said, was simply said from fear of the fire.'* Joan had just condemned herself for, having promised to no longer wear men's clothes, she was considered as *relapsed* (she had returned to sin). And only the relapsed could be sentenced to death by a court of inquisition. On the 28th and 29th of May, the twenty-eight judges unanimously declared her guilty. The president Pierre Cauchon took their decision further, declaring her a heretic, excommunicating her and sentencing her to be handed over to the secular arm.

On the 30th of May 1431, Joan was taken to the stake, wearing a dress and a hat in the shape of a mitre upon which the grounds of her sentence were written, *'Heretic, relapse, apostate, idolatress.'* The executioner set fire to the stake and at around 5 in the evening, once the fire had gone out, he noticed that her body had not entirely burned. He covered it with a mixture of sulphur oil and coal... in vain. Geoffroy Thérage, the executioner, then gathered the remains and threw them into the River Seine.

By this trial, her enemies had sought to expunge her memory: but instead, they had raised a monument.

LOOK JOAN, YOUR SACRIFICE HAS NOT BEEN IN VAIN...

IN SEPTEMBER 1435, FRANCE AND BURGUNDY WILL MAKE PEACE...

TWO YEARS LATER, CHARLES VII WILL ENTER THE RECONQUERED CITY OF PARIS...

... AND IN 1444, AFTER 30 YEARS OF OCCUPATION, THE CITY OF ROUEN WILL BE FREE.

ONCE THESE DAYS HAVE PASSED, CHARLES VII WILL ORDER AN INVESTIGATION ON YOUR TRIAL PROCEEDINGS...
... AND ON YOUR EXECUTION AT THE STAKE.
45

THOSE WHO ONCE DEFAMED YOU WILL RECONSIDER THEIR ACCUSATIONS.
TIMES WILL HAVE CHANGED. AND GRACE WILL BE YOURS.
THEY WILL ALL CALL THEIR ACTS INTO QUESTION.
AFTER LONG HOURS OF EXAMINATION AND HEARINGS, YOUR TRIAL WILL BE REVIEWED...
AND ON THE 7TH OF JULY 1456, IN ROUEN...
DONG
DONG
DO
... YOU WILL BE SOLEMNLY REHABILITATED BY THE KING HIMSELF!

YEARS WILL GO BY AND YOU WILL NEVER BE TOTALLY FORGOTTEN...

CONQUESTS, WARS AND ILLUSTRIOUS FIGURES WILL SHAPE THE NATION.

INGRATITUDE OF THE TIMES...
... OTHERS WILL BEAR THE SYMBOLS OF THIS NATION, OF THIS COUNTRY OF FRATERNITY AND LIBERTY.
AND ON THE DAWN OF THE 20TH CENTURY...
?!
JOB

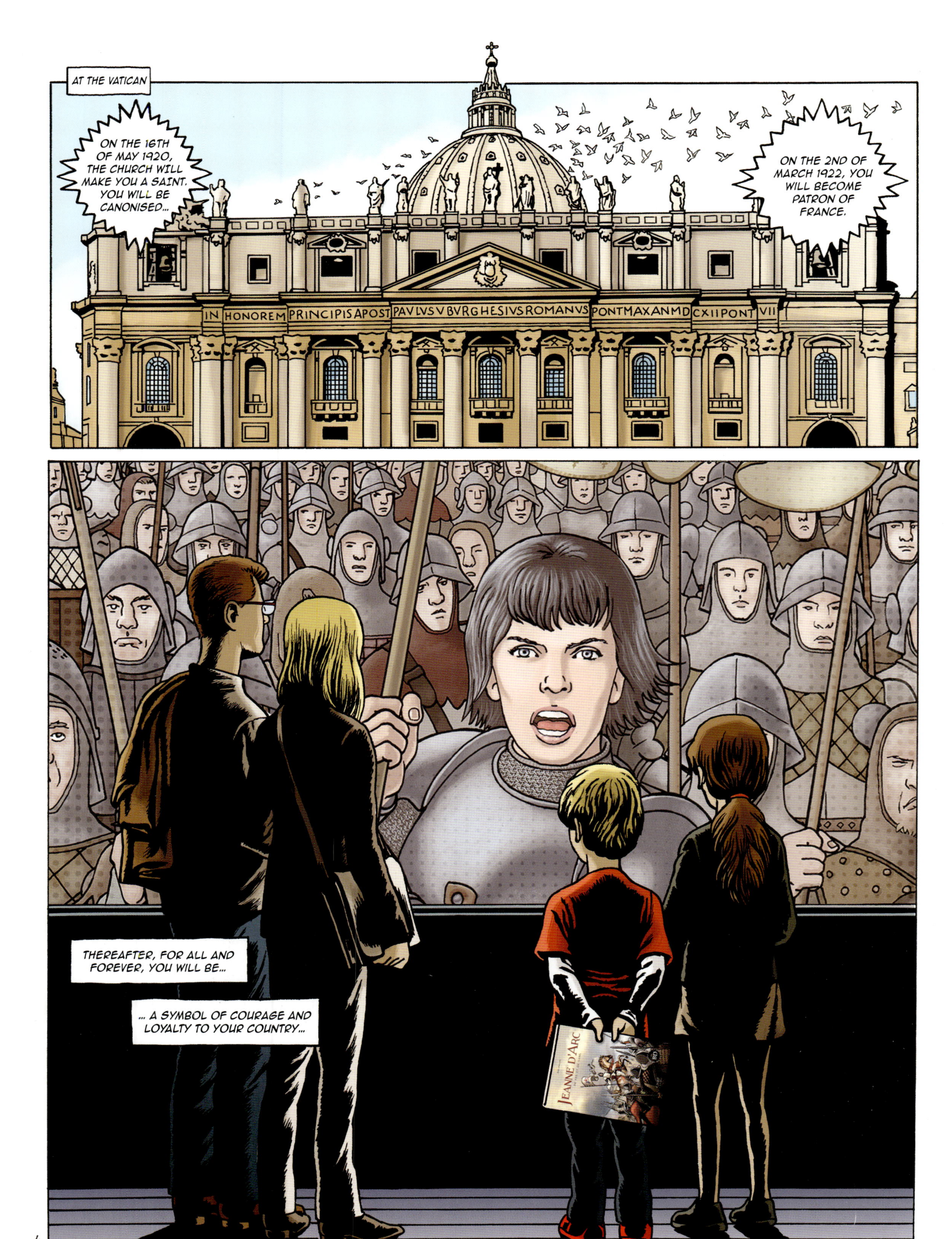
AT THE VATICAN
ON THE 16TH OF MAY 1920, THE CHURCH WILL MAKE YOU A SAINT. YOU WILL BE CANONISED...
ON THE 2ND OF MARCH 1922, YOU WILL BECOME PATRON OF FRANCE.
IN HONOREM PRINCIPIS APOST PAVLVS V BVRGHESIVS ROMANVS PONT MAX AN MDCXII PONT VII
THEREAFTER, FOR ALL AND FOREVER, YOU WILL BE...
... A SYMBOL OF COURAGE AND LOYALTY TO YOUR COUNTRY...
JEANNE D'ARC
48

The rehabilitation

After Joan's death, the war was a succession of victories and defeats for both sides. Since the beginning of the Hundred Years' War in 1337, the English and the French had been tearing each other to pieces, neither side managing to impose itself. After ninety years of war, Charles VII reorganised his council and undertook to make peace with Burgundy, via the Treaty of Arras, signed in 1435. The retrieval of French soil through Charles VII could now begin. Paris surrendered to the king and truces were signed and guaranteed by the marriage of the King of England, Henry VI, with Charles VII's niece. Charles took advantage of the truce to reorganise his army. After the Battle of Castillon in 1453, the English permanently left Bordeaux. Only Calais remained in English hands, even if the Hundred Years' War was over.

Joan's rehabilitation trial could begin at last. The judges of her first trial were among the witnesses. The evidence they then provided was essentially aimed at minimising their acts and at proclaiming their good faith and their allegiance to the King of France. The trial was held in Paris and began on the 7th of November 1455 to be concluded on the 7th of July 1456. Joan was restored to the status of a 'good Christian' and the Church acknowledged that the young woman had been unjustly sentenced by a bishop and not by the Pope and the Church.

Joan's story was, for a while, forgotten. In 1752, Voltaire wrote a 'heroi-comic poem' in which he denounced popular gullibility, the intervention of Providence in history and the criminal abuse that results from religious sectarianism. In 1805, the sub-prefect of Bergerac, Pierre Caze, chose theatre to offer his own vision of Joan. She was depicted as Charles VII's secret sister. If truth be told, this scenario was not of his own invention, but simply inspired by Shakespeare's play, *Henry VI.* These pseudo-historians are referred to as 'bastardisers'. Others, known as 'survivalists', did not believe Joan to have died at the stake in Rouen - a hypothesis supported by a number of 'fake' appearances of Joan after her death. The first bona fide historian was Jules Quicherat. From 1841 to 1849, he produced the very first scientific works based on historical sources. However, the story, at a time when no media existed, was already known to, and consquently related internationally by authors such as Voltaire – even if his poem is not at all plausible – Schiller in Germany, Mark Twain in the United States, Anatole France in France and Verdi in the opera in which he was able to transpose the depiction of the young girl fighting against the invader, in reference to the Austrians in Italy. In 1870, France had been invaded by the Prussians and needed to rid itself of the Alsace and Lorraine regions. Joan of Arc – depicted as a young girl from Lorraine (which she had never been), represented a figure who, since her death, had become a model of bravery and tenacity for all those faced with fighting the oppressor. A great number of young girls were subsequently nicknamed Joan of Arc. This worldwide recognition was not associated with her faith, but with her courage and her determination. The Church took around five hundred years to acknowledge her. The famous Bishop of Orléans, Félix Dupanloup, initiated efforts towards her recognition in 1869. Furthermore, the 1905 French law on the separation of the Church and the State was a decisive event for Joan was beatified in 1909, before being canonised in 1920. The same year, the French Republic voted a law establishing a national day, the second Sunday in May, in her honour and the project to build a national monument in Rouen. The monument, the Church of St. Joan of Arc, was built from 1973 to 1979 in Rouen's Place du Vieux-Marché. It is on a wall built close to the church that André Malraux's famous quotation is engraved, *'O Jeanne, without sepulchre, without portrait, you know that the tomb of heroes is the heart of the living.'*

JOAN OF ARC FURTHER INFORMATION

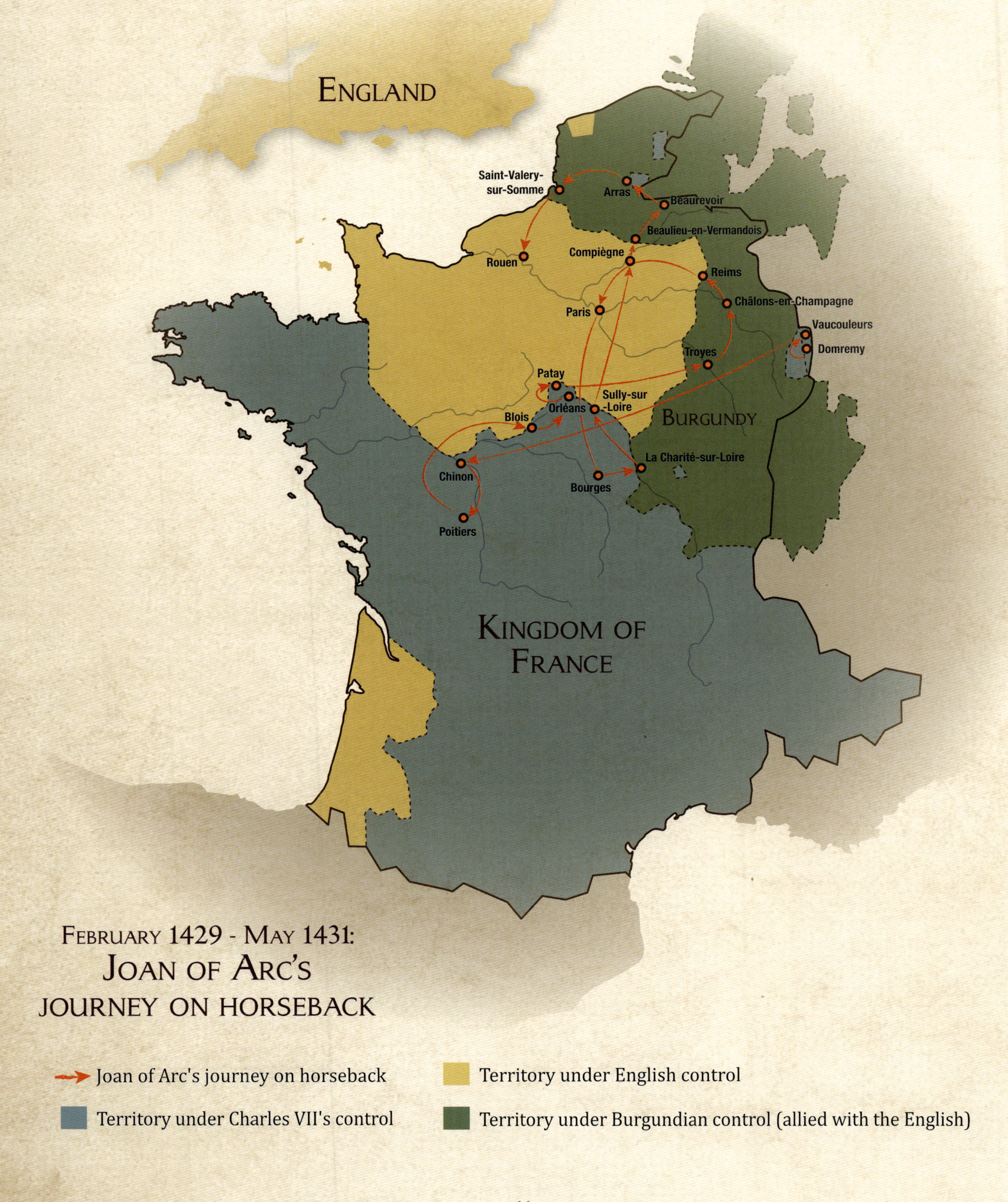

February 1429 - May 1431:
Joan of Arc's
journey on horseback

Chinon

© Christophe Raimbault-CD37

In the 15th century, the fortress of Chinon was a thousand-year-old fortified town, the characteristic outline of which stretched along the summit of a 500 metre-long rocky outcrop. Its ramparts were punctuated with defensive towers; built at different periods, they symbolised the various sovereigns who left their indelible mark on the site.
The residential quarters only adopted their permanent configuration, comprising three wings arranged around an inner courtyard, in the 15th century. At this time in history, Charles VII and his wife Marie of Anjou resided on the first floor of the southern wing of these royal apartments. It was in 1429 that Charles VII first met with Joan of Arc, in Chinon. This famous episode in the 'Johannine' epic is generally described as a mythical and miraculous scene: that of the *Recognition.* However, there is no truth in this legend for their encounter actually took place within the confines of the king's bedroom. Around a month later, Joan returned to see the king who, this time, welcomed her to the fortress's grand hall. This second audition bore the public and official characteristics that are often associated with the first. It marked the end of the Poitiers inquiry and served as Joan's official introduction to the royal court.

Beaugency

© Service patrimoine de beaugency

The statue of Joan of Arc that stands in Place Saint-Firmin was produced by Fournier in the late 19th century. It bears witness to the Maid of Orléans' passing here in 1429. The fortifications, of which many vestiges remain, render access via the now thousand-year-old bridge somewhat intimidating. The Constable Arthur de Richemont joined forces with the French besiegers. The English relinquished the city on the 17th of June. The troops then headed for Patay. The church tower chimes ring three times daily. '*My friends, what is left for such a gentle dauphin? Orléans, Beaugency, Notre-Dame de Cléry, Vendôme, Vendôme.*'

Vaucouleurs

© CDMM

From its creation during the Gallo-Roman period to this very day, via the 15th century, throughout which it played a capital role, Vaucouleurs is 'the city that armed Joan of Arc'. On the 13th of May 1428, Joan entered the castle gates for the first time to request from Baudricourt, captain to the King of France and governor of the fortified city, an escort to return to Chinon. '*Joan of Arc's relics? There are none. There never have been. [...] As such, all of France becomes a reliquary, each town and each monument, each stone ennobled by her touch becomes a relic of the great heroin. In Vaucouleurs, a site capital to her story, all that remains within the city that still bears the slightest breath of medieval times is her relic.*' The Musée Jehanne-d'Arc, a museum located within the town council walls, houses around 300 museum pieces including a fine collection of bronzes, drawings, advertising pieces, stained-glass windows, collections, etc.

ORLÉANS

© Jean-Marc Feliciano

Capital of the eponymous duchy, the town of Orléans was also the capital of the Armagnac party. Its strategic importance was all the greater since it was also situated within a major trading hub on the banks of the Loire. On the 12th of October 1428, the Earl of Salisbury set siege on the town, either to prevent the Armagnacs from attacking Paris or to secure a river route to Angers, his ultimate goal. After the fall of Rouvray on the 12th of February 1429, the town began to negotiate its surrender. Joan of Arc entered Orléans on the evening of the 29th of April, galvanising the population to such an extent that the city's commander, known as the 'Bastard of Orléans', headed immediately for Blois to raise the French army, which in turn entered the town on the 4th of May. The same day, the bastille of St. Loup, the most easterly English position, was taken. The bastille of the Augustins, to the south, followed on the 6th. On the 7th, the town bridge was cleared after recapturing the Tourelles gatehouse and, on the 8th, the English army finally retreated, having lost around a third of its men.

REIMS

© Jacques Driol

Reims, the city of anointments since Louis the Pious, was an essential destination for Joan of Arc, in a country shaken by war and conflict since around eighty years. After her victory in Orléans in May 1429, Joan of Arc walked through the Dieu-Lumière gate in Reims on the 16th of July 1429, to see the dauphin crowned the following day in Notre-Dame Cathedral. Charles VII's anointment is immortalised here in the form of a stained glass window produced by Marc Chagall in 1974, whereas Joan of Arc's passing here is symbolised by the equestrian statue that adorns the square, created by Paul Dubois in 1895. This historic event, which proffered the town with a newfound national dimension, has been commemorated by its inhabitants since 1921, via the 'Johannine fairs', organised every year in June, in the form of re-enactments and festive events. A commemorative plaque dating from 1929, installed near the Le Vergeur museum-hotel, signifies Joan of Arc's passing through Reims. A further statue by Roger de Villiers, a World Heritage Site, can be seen inside the Saint-Nicaise church.

LOCHES

© Chanel Koehl - Conseil départemental d'Indre-et-Loire

Located in the Indre valley, on the old road linking Amboise with Poitiers, the royal city of Loches is a unique heritage site that tells the tale of France's eventful history. Built on a rocky outcrop and enclosed within a two kilometre-long wall, its various construction phases stretched over five centuries (11th-16th). To the south, the city was defended by a monumental keep, built between 1013 and 1015 by the Count of Anjou, Fulk III the Black and is considered to be one of the largest and the best preserved keeps from the Roman period. To the north, a dwelling was built in the 14th century upon orders from Louis I of Anjou. The following century, it welcomed King Charles VII, who paid regular visits, choosing the site as his second-preferred fortification after Chinon. It is within these walls that, late May 1429, Joan of Arc came with John, the 'Bastard of Orléans' to meet with the dauphin, whom she exhorted to travel to Reims to '*take a worthy crown*'. Convinced by the Maid's good faith, Charles VII decided to set the royal army marching for his 'journey of anointment'.

Rouen

© Thomas Boivin

Joan of Arc's second trial, aimed at re-establishing her innocence, was held in what is now the Historial Jeanne-d'Arc. Witnesses, re-enactments and audiovisual effects plunge the spectator into the most famous of all judiciary inquiries held in Rouen, in the midst of the 15th century. From her military action to reconquer the French crown to her agony at the stake, Joan of Arc's epic and captivating story is presented throughout the medieval halls of a monument once closed to the public, and via encounters with those that have shaped its history over a holographic dialogue. This original approach offers an insight into the multiple faces of Joan of Arc. And it lifts the veil on the many myths and legends associated with her life.

Domremy-la-Pucelle

© CD88

Joan of Arc's birthplace: It was within this modest ploughman's house that Joan of Arc was born in the early 15th century, around 1412. In memory of her deeds, this house has been preserved, enhanced and decorated over the centuries with inscriptions and sculptures. The property of the Vosges Council since 1818 and a listed Historic Monument since 1840, Joan of Arc's birthplace is located within a wooded garden, in the immediate vicinity of the parish church. In 2012, it was awarded the 'Maison des Illustres' (houses of the illustrious) label. While the facade relates the building's six century history, its four simple and modestly-sized rooms invite the visitor to follow in the footsteps of a young girl, who was like so many others before she became a world-famous heroin. The 'Visages de Jehanne' visitor centre: Over a museographical trail and a variety of audiovisual tools, the 'Visages de Jehanne' centre offers an insight into the medieval period and its society, of the Hundred Years' War and a presentation on Joan's childhood and trials.

Compiègne

© Office de tourisme de l'agglomération de Compiègne

A genuine obstacle before the province of Artois, Compiègne played a major strategic role in the conflicts that opposed the Burgundians and the Armagnacs. The town was captured at least three times between 1414 and 1429. During the Anglo-Burgundian counter-offensive in 1430, Joan was sent here with 400 armed men to repeat the exemplary feat of arms she had accomplished during the Orléans siege. However, on the 23rd of May, during an outing, she found herself trapped between the Burgundians she was attacking and a group of English troops who had come to support them. Her retreat route towards the bridge over the River Oise had been cut and she was captured by sacrificing herself along with a small group of troops, in order to enable her men to board the boats that awaited them.

Chécy

The convoy of supplies for Orléans left Blois on the 27th of April 1429, largely bypassing the town to the south to avoid the English garrisons, then heading northwards to approach the Loire from upstream, opposite Chécy. The Orléans boats were to sail up the Loire, taking full advantage of favourable winds, to load provisions then to sail back down towards the town. However, that day, the winds were blowing in the wrong direction. Joan of Arc criticised the Bastard of Orléans for having made the wrong decision when the wind changed direction. This was considered by those present as a miracle, hence ensuring Joan's good repute among the royal army.

Sainte-Catherine-de-Fierbois

A particularly well-known chapel once stood in Sainte-Catherine-de-Fierbois. Built in 1373, it welcomed prisoners and other individuals facing danger of death, who came to praise St. Catherine and to leave ex-voto offerings. Joan of Arc came by here on her way to Chinon, around the 22nd of February 1429. Here, behind the altar, she had seen a sword, the blade of which bore five crosses, '*entre aulcunes vieilles ferrailles*' (among other old irons) as per the French terms of her trial proceedings. When Joan met with the dauphin Charles, just before being sent to Orléans, she had the sword recovered and restored by a blacksmith, then sent to her in Tours.

Patay

On the 18th of June 1429, on its way from Meung-sur-Loire, the French army pursued the English troops as far as Patay, where the latter had planned an ambush. However, a deer thrust into their ranks, spurring cries that alerted the French. Encouraged by the Maid of Orleans, the French launched their attack, annihilating the English army (2,000 men killed) and capturing its military staff. This battle marked a turning point in the Hundred Years' War, galvanised the French and paved the way for the future king's coronation in Reims.

Saint-Pierre-le-Moûtier

The brigand captain Perrinet Gressard had founded a small independent principality around La Charité-sur-Loire. Upon his return from the king's coronation, the seigneur of Albret, half-brother to the Grand Chamberlain of France, Georges de la Trémoille, was entrusted with recovering the region, which was far too close to Bourges where the king had established one of his capitals. Joan of Arc travelled here and a witness report by her squire Jean d'Aulon attests to her participation in the town's capture, and how she rallied the undecided as she cried '*To the fagots and hurdles all of ye, and make a bridge.*' Henceforth, the soldiers seemed to emerge from the earth and they took the town.

Neufchâteau

Neufchâteau, which boasts the finest of historic heritage, stands on a rocky promontory in the heart of the Vosges plain, just 10 kilometres from Domremy-la-Pucelle, our heroin's birthplace. During the Hundred Years' War, to flee the Burgundians, Joan sought refuge in the Cordeliers convent in Neufchâteau from August to October 1428.
The square, Place Jeanne d'Arc (and the statue by Charles Pêtre dating from 1859), where the town's old streets converge, offers fine proof of the extent to which this saint is worshiped in and around her childhood village.

Beaulieu-les-Fontaines

'After brief days, sent her under good escort, to his castle in Baulieu', Perceval de Cagny, Jean d'Alençon's chronicler tells us. Joan of Arc was taken prisoner before Compiègne on the 23rd of May 1430 and conducted to Beaulieu castle around the 25th. It was during this stage in her journey to Rouen that she first attempted to escape. However, she was recaptured, *'It does not please God that I escape this time.'* She was locked inside a dungeon, located under a military hall in one of the castle towers.

Cléry-Saint-André

The town of Cléry and its collegiate church were pillaged and burnt down by the English army upon its arrival on the banks of the Loire around the 25th of September 1428. Considered as a great sacrilege, this event later led to the death of the Earl of Salisbury who was killed on the 3rd of November the same year, in Orléans. Joan of Arc probably travelled by Cléry on the 29th of April 1429, with the supply convoy on its way to Orléans.

Jargeau

The town had been captured by the English on the 5th of October 1428. On the 11th of June 1429, after raising the Orléans siege, the French prepared to recapture the town, which was under the nominal command of the Duke of Alençon, who was known to be rather timorous. Once the French artillery had broken through the city walls, Joan of Arc had to admonish him several times before he finally gave orders to attack. The assault was so violent that the Earl of Suffolk, the English captain in control of the town, did not even have the time to escape. Pursued and caught by a squire, he dubbed him before surrendering, so that he would at least have the consolation of having been captured by a knight.

Meung-sur-Loire

After Joan of Arc had delivered Orléans on the 8th of May 1429, the English then concentrated their troops in Meung-sur-Loire, the bridge of which was of major strategic importance at the time. On the 14th of June, after recapturing Jargeau, Joan of Arc told the Duke of Alençon, *'Tomorrow after dinner, I wish to go and see those at Meung.'* On the 15th of June, the French arrived from the left bank of the Loire, attacking and taking control of the fortified bridge, chasing the English out of the town and its castle which had served as their headquarters since September 1428.

Lagny-sur-Marne

© Bernard Minoret

Three times, Joan of Arc chose the safety of the fortified town of Lagny-sur-Marne, which had remained forever loyal to the King of France. On the 12th of September 1429, after the failed attack on Paris, she stopped over here with the king and his army. Then, from the 5th to the 7th of April 1430, when what was to be presented during her trial as the 'Miracle of Lagny' took place: Joan joined a group of young girls in prayer to beg the Virgin to bring a three day-old baby, said to be dead, back to life. The child then yawned three times – just long enough for him to be baptised. After travelling to Melun on the 17th or the 18th of April, she returned to Lagny to fight the Anglo-Burgundians on the Vaires plain.

Mehun-sur-Yèvre

© Serv. cult. Mehun - mus. Charles VII ; coll. Ph. Bon

After John of Berry, Charles VII also chose Mehun-sur-Yèvre castle as his favourite retreat in times of political and military unrest. He was proclaimed king in 1422 among a number of his partisans. In Mehun, he organised states general, housed his family, comprised his court, but, above all, he welcomed Joan of Arc to the castle's ceremonial room to present her with her letters of ennoblement. Letters which, most probably, only served to seal his own power. It was upon the Christmas of 1429, 'la Noël', between the feats of Reims and Compiègne, that Joan was at the height of her glory and the king enjoyed renewed confidence. Joan of Arc never lived in the castle, nor did she in any other royal residence. She was accommodated in town in the Grant-Maison, a fine private residence belonging Renault Thierry, the king's surgeon and physicist.

Gien

© PackShot - Fotolia

It was during her first journey to Gien, in February 1429, that news of Joan of Arc's arrival began to spread, in Orléans in particular. For the town bordered with Burgundy. This is where the army that was to take Charles VII to Reims for his coronation was gathered. Joan of Arc arrived here directly from Patay on the 25th of June. She left on the 29th, to launch the campaign that would lead to the recovery of the entire Champagne region and a vast share of the Paris basin.